Eucalyptus Saligna   Radiata Pine   Purpleheart   White Ash   Red Oak

English Pine   Purpleheart   Pearwood   Eucalyptus   Red Oak   Douglas Fir   Redwood   E

nut   White Ash   Macassar Ebony   Red Oak   Douglas Fir   Redwood   Honduras Maho

ras Mahogany   Eucalyptus Saligna   Radiata Pine   White Oak   Butternut   Lodgepol

Pine   Purpleheart   Pearwood   European Walnut   Amaranth   Pearwood   White Bir

Red Oak   Lodgepole Pine   Cedar   Mahogany   Eucalyptus   Eastern White Pine

Pine   English Pine   Purpleheart   Pearwood   White Birch   Teak   Macassar Ebony

nut   White Ash   Macassar Ebony   Red Oak   Douglas Fir   Redwood   Eastern White P

DESIGNING WITH

WOOD

The Creative Touch

Carol Soucek King, Ph.D.

Foreword by Stanley Abercrombie, FAIA

Interior Details

AN IMPRINT OF
PBC INTERNATIONAL, INC.

Distributor to the book trade in the United States and Canada
Rizzoli International Publications Inc.
300 Park Avenue South
New York, NY 10010

Distributor to the art trade in the United States and Canada
PBC International, Inc.
One School Street
Glen Cove, NY 11542

Distributor throughout the rest of the world
Hearst Books International
1350 Avenue of the Americas
New York, NY 10019

Library of Congress Cataloging-in-Publication Data

King, Carol Soucek.
    Designing with wood : the creative touch / by Carol Soucek King.
        p. cm.
        Includes index.
        ISBN 0-86636-329-7 (hb : alk. paper).
        1. Wood in interior decoration. 2. Architectural woodwork.
    I. Title.
NK2115.5.W66K56   1995   95-13001
728—dc20   CIP

CAVEAT— Information in this text is believed accurate, and will pose no
problem for the student or casual reader. However, the author was often
constrained by information contained in signed release forms, information
that could have been in error or not included at all. Any misinformation
(or lack of information) is the result of failure in these attestations. The
author has done whatever is possible to insure accuracy.

Designed by Garrett Schuh

Color separation by
Fine Arts Repro House Co., Ltd., H.K.
Printing and binding by
Toppan Printing Co. (H.K.) Ltd. Hong Kong

10 9 8 7 6 5 4 3 2 1

Printed in China

To Creativity at Home...

and Being at Home with Creativity!

Cedar   California Redwood   Red Oa[k]

White Oak   Butternut   Red Alder   Walnut   Rock Maple   Eastern White Pine   Englis[h]

[Europea]n Walnut   Amaranth   European Cherry   Akatio   White Birch   Teak   French Walnu[t]

[W]estern Red Cedar   [Ca]lifornia Redwood   Red Oak   Lodgepole Pine   Cedar   Hondura[s]

[Ald]er   Amaranth   American Black Walnut   Rock Maple   Eastern White Pine   English P[ine]

[Europea]n Cherry   Akatio   White Birch   Teak   French Walnut   White Ash   Macassar Ebony

White Oak   Butternut   Red Alder   American Black Walnut   Rock Maple   Eastern

[Europea]n Walnut   Amaranth   European Cherry   Akatio   White Birch   Teak   French Walnut

FOREWORD

Stanley Abercrombie, FAIA, *Chief Editor*, INTERIOR DESIGN

Sorry to repeat myself, but in the last sentence of a book titled *A Philosophy of Interior Design*, I wrote that interiors constitute "our most personal art." Carol Soucek King, I'm glad to see, seems to share the same view, for the admirable series of books Dr. King has planned promises to focus on just those aspects of interior design that make it personal.

The grand concept is not to be neglected, of course. Like any other art, interior design depends for its success on the encompassing vision that relates its many elements in a meaningful whole. But such vision, in interiors, becomes manifest and comprehensible through the medium of myriad details with which we are in intimate contact: the feel of a drawer-pull, the profile of a cornice, the polish and grain of wood, the "hand" of fabric.

This contact involves all our senses. We see our interiors, certainly, but we also smell the materials in them, we hear their acoustic properties, we brush up against their walls, step on their floors, open their casegoods, sit on their chairs. More than any other, interior design is the art we use. In that sense, it is not only our most personal art, but also the one most responsible for our well-being. In the context of increasingly brutalized urban environments, this is increasingly true and increasingly important. Interior design is often our refuge.

It is therefore a very welcome prospect that Dr. King is turning her experienced editorial eye to the details and materials on which the art of interior design depends. I'm sure we will all benefit from her discoveries.

PREFACE

From the beginning of time, wood has been used to provide shelter for humankind. Whether locally grown or imported from foreign lands, this vibrantly natural material is treasured around the world both as a structural material and for finishing of all kinds — for wood makes people feel comfortable!

In showing how wood has been used residentially with much magnificence and great innovation, I have endeavored to capture its warmth and beauty as well as illuminate the styles and techniques employed by the architects, interior designers and mastercraftsmen responsible for its execution. Through my work on this book, it has become all the more evident to me that wood is valued as a resource because of its seemingly endless varieties and their breadth of color, grain and density. It is also resilient — it gives. It is adaptable — it moves and breathes with the climate.

Through visits to houses and apartments, newly built and remodeled, I've discovered a wide variety of styles and periods that incorporate an even broader variety of woods and finishes. Some reveal traditional methods of working with wood, others are rich in new ideas for ceilings, flooring, moldings, paneling and freestanding furniture. I hope the reader will find among them inspiration to bring still more homes alive with wood.

— *Carol Soucek King,* Ph.D.

INTRODUCTION

Joseph A. Sorrelli, *1993-94 President,* ARCHITECTURAL WOODWORK INSTITUTE

Some years ago the famous architect Frank Lloyd Wright said, "Wood is a friend of mine. The best friend on earth of man is the tree. When we use the tree respectfully and economically, we have one of the great resources of the earth. It is a beautiful material, friendly to man, the supreme material for his dwelling purposes. If a man is going to live, he should live with wood."

As the years have passed, Wright's words carry even more weight today. In an era of environmental consciousness, wood is recognized as the only renewable commonly used building material. Wood offers a rich variety of textures, colors and appearances, and infinite possibilities of shapes. Its characteristics, including an ability to be worked in many ways, have given us a rich flexibility in building everything from very small pieces of furniture to huge auditoriums. We have grown accustomed to living with wood in all aspects of our lives, and wood has made our lives richer.

Woodworkers and their suppliers recognize the special position wood holds, and they have worked hard to extend and maintain this valuable resource. Wood producers have pledged to practice sustainable forestry to meet today's forest resource needs without compromising the ability of future generations to meet their own needs. The industry is committed to practicing a forest stewardship ethic that integrates the growing, nurturing and harvesting of trees for useful products with the conservation of soil, air and water quality, and wildlife and fish habitat.

Woodworkers themselves have taken important steps to maximize the utilization of our renewable resource. Veneers today are much thinner than they were in previous years, allowing us to obtain more from each tree. Computerized machinery allows us to minimize waste in woodworking, and steps ranging from thinner saw blades utilizing newer materials, to recycling more of the products of woodwork that were formerly considered waste material, have increased our productive capabilities while allowing us to contribute to the movement toward sustainable forest management.

The use of wood to create everything from simple habitat to finely crafted woodwork traces its origins almost to the dawn of humankind. In spite of its rich history, we continue to discover new ways to use it and new forms to create from it. Its artistic capabilities as well as its adaptability for our living needs are unlimited. From simple framing behind the walls of houses, to dramatic use of the colors and textures of wood veneers and molding on walls, stairs, ceilings and openings, wood has made itself indispensable to us in many ways. As you read through Dr. King's book, consider all the ways wood touches your own life. Perhaps you'll agree with Frank Lloyd Wright, "Wood is a friend of mine."

Cedar   *California Redwood*   Red C

White Oak   Butternut   *Red Alder*   *Walnut*   Rock Maple   *Eastern White Pine*   Eng

ean Walnut   *Amaranth*   *European Cherry*   *Akatio*   White   *rench Walnu*

Western Red Cedar   *California Redwood*   *Red Oak*   *Lodgepole Pine*   *Cedar*   *Hondur*

der   Amaranth   *American Black Walnut*   Rock Maple   *Eastern White Pine*   English

ean Cherry   *Akatio*   *White Birch*   *Teak*   *French Walnut*   White Ash   *Macassar Ebon*

White Oak   Butternut   *A   rican Black Walnut*   *Rock Maple*   *Easter*

ean Wal t   *Amaranth*   *European Cherry*   *Akatio*   *White Birch*   *Teak*   *French Waln*

Lodgepole Pine   Cedar   Honduras Mahogany   *Eucalyptus Saligna*   Radiata Pine

Pine   Purpleheart   Pearwood   *Eucalyptus*   Red Oak   Douglas Fir   *Redwood*   Euca

White Ash   Macassar Ebony   Red Oak   Douglas Fir   Redwood   *Honduras Mahogany*

Mahogany   Eucalyptus Saligna   Radiata Pine   White Oak   B   *dgepole Pin*

e   Purpleheart   Butternut   *European Walnut*   Amaranth   Pearwood   *White Birch*

Red Oak   Lodgepole Pine   *Cedar*   Mahogany   Eucalyptus   Eastern White Pine   *Wh*

White Pine   English Pine   *Purplehe*   Pearwood   *White Birch*   *Teak*   *Macassar Ebo*

White Ash   *Macassar Ebony*   Red Oak   Douglas Fir   *Redwood*   Eastern White Pine

IN HARMONY WITH NATURE

Douglas Fir, Redwood, Yellow Pine &
Western Red Cedar

Capturing the spirit and the form of a site's original natural beauty is often the greatest challenge facing architect, interior designer or home owner, and often the answer lies in wood. Thus it was for Henry Whiting II, whose main home was designed with great sensitivity to the land by Frank Lloyd Wright. In planning this, his second home, he turned to architect **Bart Prince**. Whiting knew that he wanted a primarily wood house for the panoramic site — twelve softly sculpted acres nestled between gently rolling mountains and hills in Sun Valley, Idaho. Yet he also felt that mimicking the area's so-called "regional" log and wood structures simply would not do. He determined that, above everything

ABOVE *In the living room, the built-in seating is made of clear Douglas fir, as are the windowsill and the light-shelf above the glass.*

Photography by Alan Weintraub

ABOVE *The house stretches out over the landscape rather than being centered in a confined structure, allowing for the separation of the master suite at one end and guest rooms at the other. Each section has its own spectacular view of the valley and mountains without being exposed to the rest of the house. Curving walls are of split-face masonry. The roof is covered in Western red cedar shingles, with every other row doubled to emphasize the horizontal line.*

RIGHT *A horizontal curve of glue-laminated Douglas fir defines the low-ceiling entry, which serves as preamble to the high, skylighted space of the living room. The windowsill is clear Douglas fir. The dark, screened space between the beam and cedar shingles is for the "cold roof" which keeps the snow from melting in winter.*

A projecting beam of glue-laminated Douglas fir protects the walkway and the angled glazed enclosure from glare.

else, his home would reflect its surroundings to the greatest extent possible — its grace, its joy and its uniqueness.

As the architect, known for his biomorphic-naturescapes, comments, "This design could only have been expressed using wood."

GLUE-LAMINATED BEAMS: *Western Wood Structures, Inc.*

OPPOSITE & ABOVE *Over the living/dining area, the tongue-and-groove yellow pine decking covers Douglas fir beams that are joined by a large, curving glue-laminated beam made of architectural-grade structural Douglas fir. Support members of the skylight are redwood. The horizontal light-shelf above the glass is clear fir. Two serpentine masonry walls extend in either direction to enclose the bedrooms at both ends of the house. The stone path emphasizes the separation between the formal and informal spaces.*

ABOVE *The master bathroom opens onto tongue-and-groove yellow pine decking spanning the space between the beams. Trim pieces are in clear Douglas fir.*

CELEBRATING, NOT ELABORATING

Douglas Fir & Western Red Cedar

This remodel in the Washington Park area of Seattle provided architect *James W. P. Olson* with the opportunity to update a house that he designed as an architect in 1964 and built in 1970. It already provided much that the client, artist Ann Buckner, valued — especially the sense of surprise afforded by every view and vista.

The heart of the project was the addition of a garden room which acts as both entry and an outlook to a central courtyard. The project's soul is the celebration of wood in its natural state, a contemporary version of simple wood frame construction, which is traditional in the Northwest.

CONTRACTOR AND CUSTOM WOODWORK: *Jerry Fulks and Company/Michael Suver*
GENERAL CONTRACTOR: *Matheny Construction*
CUSTOM WOODWORK: *Sea Ranch Cabinets/Bob Little*
CEDAR SIIDING: *Healdsburg Lumber*

The treatment of wood is the key to the way this home harmonizes with the heavily wooded site's original tree-laden beauty. The exterior Western red cedar has been stained the same soft driftwood hue as the interior Douglas fir, unifying the living spaces with the outdoors.

Photography by Michael Jensen

Almost in the manner of traditional Japanese design, the architect's use of fir and cedar celebrates wood's natural state with as little elaboration as possible.

The understated use of brass-plated metal detailing acts as just the right touch of "jewlery" in much the same way as the detailing on the owner's collection of antique furniture, which has been placed by interior designer David Weatherford.

NEW TUNE FOR SUNDANCE

Western Red Cedar & California Redwood

Residing congenially amid the alpine community of Sundance, Utah, is a contemporary residence completely in harmony with its more rustic and traditional neighbors. Due to the efforts of architect **Dwight Hooker** and designer **Lenny Steinberg**, Judy Polone's home, engineered around a mountain ledge with a triangular atrium encircling a grand old pine tree, preserves the forest in fact and feeling.

BELOW *The collection of California redwood furniture, created by Steinberg with her associate Melinda Ring, expands on the structure's elements. Since the cedar was clad horizontally, she stressed the same horizontality in the furnishings, as well as in the cedar and redwood wine cellar.*

Photography by Andrew Bush

LEFT *The inviting spa is of exposed tongue-and-groove, smooth-sawn, inland Western red cedar.*

BELOW & OPPOSITE *The exterior is clad in six-inch tongue-and-groove lightly roughed Western red cedar. The "V" groove, when used on the rough side, makes a flush connection. The outdoor redwood furniture was designed by Lenny Steinberg with Sarah Binder.*

CONTRACTOR: **Bert Thomas**
LUMBER: **A & Y Lumber**
OUTDOOR REDWOOD FURNITURE: **Lenny Steinberg and Sarah Binder, hand made by Eliza and Raanan Harel**
REDWOOD DINING TABLE AND CABIN-LIKE WINE CELLAR: **Lenny Steinberg and associate Melinda Ring, handmade by Eliza and Raanan Harel**
LAMINATE AND LEATHER CHAIRS: **Lenny Steinberg and associate Melinda Ring**

CALIFORNIA CLASSIC

California Redwood & Douglas Fir

This 3,300-square-foot residence, originally designed by Buff, Straub & Hensman (now **Buff, Smith & Hensman**) in 1959 in San Marino, California, was carefully planned to relate to its natural site, to save all major existing trees and to take advantage of the view across the canyon to the west.

The structure, made of resawn clear-heart California redwood siding, Douglas fir structural members, stucco and Norman brick paving, is an excellent example of post-and-beam construction influenced by the craftsman houses of Greene and Greene and the traditional Japanese, with a touch of Frank Lloyd Wright. Yet it makes its own strong architectural statement.

ABOVE *During restoration and remodeling, the wood decks, trellis and steps were completely replaced with thicker prestained Douglas fir decking, beams and treads.*

LEFT *A yellow pole juts jauntily through the purity of the evenly spaced clerestory beams.*

Photography by Rick Barnes

The structure is organized on a thirty-two-inch module which facilitates economic framing techniques and is expressed in the size of the doors and windows as well as the distance between the exposed California redwood rafters.

Contemporary furniture and artwork are placed in deliberate contrast to the regional craftsman structure. The owner's own wood sculpture and mobile are displayed in a pebbled rock garden which continues indoors and spills over onto the living room carpet.

LEFT *Large clerestories run the length of all rooms, allowing soft natural light to filter in, while broad overhangs shield against sun and glare.*

ABOVE *The sleek contemporary furniture is arranged on a slightly angular axis, which, along with the whimsically placed yellow pole, gives a kinetic excitement to the space.*

Sculptor Alex Moseley and his wife Jaylene purchased the home in 1985, and asked Donald C. Hensman to restore it to its original mint condition, but with some modifications. Interior designer **Bob Moore** worked in collaboration with the architect.

LOG HOME, LIGHT TOUCH

Lodgepole Pine, Western Red Cedar, Red Oak, Honduras Mahogany & Yellow Pine

The greatest challenge in building a home with tree trunks cut right from the land is to maintain the integrity of log home construction while ensuring that the extensive use of logs does not make the home seem unbearably heavy. Florida designer **Louis Shuster**, summoned north to work wonders with truckloads of unfinished lodgepole pine logs and "chinking," the grouting material used between the logs, escaped that overly woody pitfall by various inventive solutions. He used a natural taupey-beige stain for interior logs. Randomly laid planks of red oak for the floors and various custom furnishings made of red oak veneer plywood were pickled a hue intentionally lighter than the log walls. Also lightening the look as well as heightening its drama are terra cotta, river rock, weathered iron and ceramic tile.

ABOVE *To alleviate an overly woody look, the designer used custom iron details on door straps, sconces and even a mirror that he created from rebars left after construction.*

LEFT *After log home manufacturer Alpine provided his client with rudimentary architectural plans and logs — but not windows, doors, fireplace specifications or plumbing and electrical — Louis Shuster had his work cut out for him. The finish color for the logs as well as the chinking had to be selected.*

RIGHT *The tremendous use of wood, which includes log walls, oak floors and cedar ceilings, is integrated with Mexican terra-cotta floors and river rock on the two-sided fireplace and the base of the bar.*

Photography by Kim Sargent

The client's extraordinary collection of French poster art is so colorful that the designer intentionally kept the rest of the palette primarily neutral.

In the breakfast room and adjoining kitchen, wrought-iron elements, lacquered wood and ceramic tile provide a light, bright change of pace.

"It's ironic," says Shuster, "but since it is a given that every wall, window frame and door is wood, the choice of materials other than wood is one of the most important aspects in designing a log house!"

To avoid future maintenance where possible, special sealants were used on most wood finishes. Area carpets were specified in strategic places where traffic patterns on wood surfaces are greatest. All exterior log railings and Honduras mahogany decks were stripped, sanded, pressure-cleaned and sealed to protect against rain, snow and chilly northern temperatures, and the chinking was also sealed. Only the logs themselves, following the staining process, were left untouched, so they could weather naturally and thereby retain the traditional look of an old log home.

WOODWORK CONTRACTORS: *Frank J. Zadlo Construction Services, Inc.*
CUSTOM CABINETRY (OTHER THAN IN KITCHEN): *Serini Custom Woodworking*
CUSTOM WOOD FLOORS AND EXTERIOR WOOD TRIM: *George Geppert Lumber Company*
LACQUERED-WOOD KITCHEN CABINETS: *Niece Lumber Co.*
WOOD-FRAMED WINDOWS AND FRENCH DOORS: *Pella Window Co.*
CUSTOM INTERIOR AND FRONT DOORS: *Santa Fe Heritage Door Co.*
LOGS: *Alpine Log Homes*

In the dining room, antler chandeliers and a table made from one twelve-foot-long plank, of Dade County (yellow) pine, on stone bases carry out the traditional theme. To further lighten the look, Shuster made the buffet of white-painted stucco and only used oak for the edging.

REFUGE IN TRANSVAAL

Eucalyptus Saligna & Radiata Pine

Veronique Sharp's large painting of a Swazi princess fits well in "La Lavande," the second home she designed with her husband, **Colin Sharp**, publisher of South Africa's sleek interior design magazine, *Habitat*. Located in Kosmos on a lake northwest of Johannesburg in the province of Transvaal, this typical bushveld house is not only traditional to Africa but also appropriately exotic. For Mrs. Sharp, who is also known as the Madagascar-born French artist Cigale, and her husband are devoted to making others aware of the beautiful and the unusual. In this cottage they have done it again.

The project was the unification of a number of rondavels, the type of circular, thatched-roof, single-room cottage that was built in the 1940s in the traditional African pole-and-thatch manner. A central living area was built connecting four rondavels, roofed first with tiles and subsequently with thatch.

The poles used are Eucalyptus saligna, a tree that was introduced to South Africa

In addition to the eucalyptus poles and lathes and pine flooring on the mezzanine, other woods are seen in a variety of furniture, mostly old South African country examples based on English designs. Floors are black slate or are carpeted with coir, both of which are native to South Africa. Walls are roughly plastered and whitewashed. The large painting of a Swazi princess is by Cigale.

Photography by Colin Sharp

almost a century ago from Australia, where it is known as blue gum. The poles are treated with creosote/carbolynium to prevent insects and wood borers from destroying them, a protection especially important when the poles are embedded in the ground as supports. The thatching lathes, supports for the reeds, are slender branches of the same wood.

The thatch is exposed inside the house and lit after dark with halogen spotlights. The same timber is used for the balustrading inside and outside, and South African tongue-and-groove radiata pine with natural stain is used for the mezzanine floor.

A double thatched-roof extension projects from the main roof in the front to create a generous covered entertainment area, most suitable here where the climate is subtropical for eight months of the year. This second thatched roof is supported by gum poles used horizontally and vertically. Furniture here is locally made rattan. The floor is of locally fired terra-cotta tiles.

MEDITERRANEAN SUNSCREEN

Cedar

Despite numerous innovative twists that make it seem as if much dramatic license has been taken for art's sake alone, projects by Transit Design are always grounded in the basic idea that function and decoration are inseparable. In this particular home, a Mediterranean house on the Gulf of Gaeta, the way architects **Giovanni Ascarelli, Maurizio Macciocchi, Evaristo Nicolao** and **Danilo Parisio** have treated the windows and doors as a series of rolling grates provides an excellent example. These thick grilles of cedar are used as a leitmotif throughout the house, their vertical and horizontal lines contrasting with the architecture's other volumetric shapes and their latticework creating a play of light across the earthy terra-cotta floors, white stucco walls and large earthenware jars. Yet the grilles are equally functional, too, as they serve to screen the interior from the harsh midday sun without blocking the view — once again demonstrating the Transit philosophy that there are no boundaries between art and good design.

CEDAR WINDOW SCREENS: *Fabricated by Poldo Punzo*

For grilles over the windows, cedar was chosen for its characteristics of lightness and high resin content, which make it resistant to seaside weather conditions and therefore a material commonly used in the Neapolitan coastal areas and on the islands of Ischia, Procida and Capri. It was finished with a clear, impregnable lacquer, which was brushed on.

Photography by Giovanna Piemonti and Janos Grapow

Cedar California Redwood Red Oa

White Oak Butternut Red Alder Walnut Rock Maple Eastern White Pine Englis

n Walnut Amaranth European Cherry Akatio White Bir nch Walnut

Western Red Cedar California Redwood Red Oak Lodgepole Pine Cedar Hondure

er Amaranth American Black Walnut Rock Maple Eastern White Pine English

n Cherry Akatio White Birch Teak French Walnut White Ash Macassar Ebony

White Oak Butternut Red rican lack Walnut Rock Maple Eastern Wh

Walnut Amaranth European Cherry Akatio White Birch Teak nch Walnut

Lodgepole Pine Cedar *Honduras Mahogany* Eucalyptus Saligna Radiata Pine P

ine *Purpleheart* Pearwood Eucalyptus *Red Oak* Redwood Eucaly

White Ash *Macassar Ebony* Red Oak Douglas Fir *Redwood* Honduras Mahogany

Eucalyptus Saligna Radiata Pine White Oak Butternut Lodgepole Pin

Purpleheart Pearwood European Walnut Amaranth Pearwood White Birch

d Oak Lodgepole Pine Cedar ogany *Eucalyptus* Eastern White Pin

Pin *English Pine* Purpleheart Pearwood White Birch Teak Macassar Ebony

Whi Ash Macassar Eb y *Red Oak* Douglas r Redw Eastern White Pine

Maybeck Revisited

Oriented Fir Strandboard, Red Oak, Yellow Pine & California Redwood

When a 1920s-era Spanish Colonial Revival structure in Northern California was lost in a fire in 1991, the home owner turned to Ace Architects' **David Weingarten** and **Lucia Howard** for help. Since their client is a newspaper publisher, it seemed appropriate for the architects to take their inspiration from the 1899 Hearst Hall, a women's gymnasium by Bernard Maybeck, the greatest practitioner of the First Bay Region style. Named after another California publisher, in 1922, it too was consumed by fire.

The new house, just large enough to answer the needs of the client and her daughter, holds a busy street at arm's length while curling around a sunny backyard patio. Inside, there is but one main space,

LEFT *The vault ribs are exposed and finished with oriented strandboard paneling, made of refuse wood chips that have been pressed together and which the designers then chose to stain yellow.*

Photography by Alan Weintraub

ABOVE *Constructed from two-by-four-inch Douglas fir boards, the ribs have been bolted together and sheathed in oriented strandboard that was stained various hues prior to installation. The floor is kiln-dried red oak. The railing is stain-grade yellow pine, a construction-grade pine with knots that the designers deemed permissible, as the wood was to be stained.*

BELOW *Polychromatically stained oriented strandboard panels complete the main room's gothic feeling. The fireplace surround is made of copper tiles around a terra-cotta trim rescued from the house that burned. Copper shingles rise to the vaulted walls above the painted wood mantel.*

yet it is major. A vaulted great room with wooden rib supports sheathed in stained oriented strandboard, it soars to an expansive height. This paneling, with a striking texture that becomes ever more apparent when stained, holds myriad hues, which are also inspired by Maybeck. The result may as well be a stage for a gothic romance.

WOOD SUPPLIER: *Truitt & White Lumber Company*

ABOVE & LEFT *Copper-clad asphalt shingles, painted rough-sawn California redwood and a dragon-like redwood trellis provide a joyful look for the home's exterior.*

41

COUNTRY FRENCH IN CALIFORNIA

White Oak, Butternut & Red Alder

Carefully selected and expertly worked woods exude warmth throughout every room in the Charles R. and Joann Anderson residence in Pasadena, California. Working directly with the owners to achieve an interior reminiscent of an eighteenth-century country French home, **Marjorie A. Bedell** and **Lawrence G. Laughlin** of Bedell-Laughlin Associates contacted mastercraftsman Michael Haring, a cabinet-maker trained in Provence, to bring their ideas to realization. They knew that his artistry would make one yearn to reach out and caress every hand-carved and hand-finished surface.

ALL MILLWORK: *Michael Haring*

In the library, distressed white oak flooring, pegged and grooved, leads to a Louis XV-style fireplace mantel surrounded by richly detailed walls of hand-carved, hand-stained and hand-rubbed butternut paneling.

Photography by Anthony Peres

ABOVE *In the dining room, the designers asked craftsman Michael Haring to reproduce an eighteenth-century serving table in distressed red alder. The hand-carved mirror is black walnut.*

RIGHT *Upstairs, a museum reproduction of an eighteenth-century blanket chest, in white oak with raised diamond panels, holds within and without watercolors and painting supplies of the client, Southern California artist Joann Anderson.*

Save for the appliances, this kitchen might well have been created in the eighteenth century it evokes. The white oak cabinetry was carved by hand, the white oak beams were shaped by a hand-held adz and further distressed by hand, and the floor's marble tiles were set within oak pickets that have been beveled and distressed by hand. Complementing the French farmhouse look are sponged and textured walls and a mud-and-straw ceiling.

GOTHIC REVIVAL

Yellow Pine, Poplar, Rock Maple, American Black Cherry & White Oak

These two homes designed by Centerbrook Architects revel in the eccentricities of the Gothic Revival, Victorian, Shaker and American Craftsman houses found in certain Eastern U.S. coastal towns. At one, **Mark Simon** and **Leonard J. Wyeth** begin their own Gothic theme with a crooked, stumbling picket fence at the approach to the gabled courtyard and carry it through to the balanced chaos of the rooms within. In the second home, architects Simon and **James C. Childress,** working with interior designer **Michael La Rocca,** mix idioms from Nantucket shipwrights' houses, Victorian cottages and Gothic manors until any one of them would seem conventional in comparison. In both, the ideas are carried out with one of the materials most appropriate to these styles — wood.

ABOVE *The high-ceilinged space of a living room's rolling ellipse is made to feel cozier with a wreath-like cornice of simple painted poplar sticks, Southern yellow pine board, and a warmly hued coffee table of yellow pine plywood laminated with copper. Up a few steps in the rectangular dining room, a table designed by Mark Simon continues the theme with its stickwork legs. The table is made of burly rock maple veneer with an edge of American black cherry.*

Photography by Timothy Hursley

LEFT *In the kitchen/family room, the Shaker style is emphasized in the cabinets of solid rift-cut white oak which has a custom-fumed finish (a coloring process using mordants and dyes to produce a fixed color in the wood's fiber). This wood gives warmth to an otherwise modern and efficient kitchen.*

Photography by Jeff Goldberg/ESTO

In the entry to this summer home, arched openings to the stairway and second floor balcony convey a Gothic feeling, whereas wood trim made of standard rectangular lumber, crisscrossed like a rustic basket, reflects an American Craftsman tone. Hanging from the center of the domed ceiling is a chandelier made of similar sticks of wood. The wood trim is paint-grade poplar that was steam-bent on site. The floor is made of narrow boards of quarter-sawn, tongue-and-groove white oak.

Photography by Jeff Goldberg/ESTO

PAST PERFECT

Honduras Mahogany & White Oak

Mexican designer ***Samuel Sandler*** follows one muse — and she is the soul of everything classical. This is but one of the many homes in which he has imparted his belief that exquisitely detailed ornamentation in the manner of yesteryear's greatest periods of artistic achievement ennobles and enriches life.

"I believe that the ornamentation helps people relate to their surroundings and live happily," says Sandler. "In this case, wood was an ideal material with which to build the cabinets as well as the ornamentation, such as the pilasters and niches, and it was excellent for the floor, especially to make the Greek key motif. In this case as always, wood enabled us to create interesting rooms for our clients, giving them the exact look they wanted."

To re-create a traditional English reading room in a new home in Mexico, Honduras mahogany was selected for all cabinetry as well as pilasters and paneling. The niche for the desk was created from several pieces of solid mahogany. The white oak floor, stained to match the mahogany, is embellished with the Greek key design used profusely throughout the house.

Photography by Michael Carvajal

IN THE EDWARDIAN MANNER

American Black Cherry, Honduras
Mahogany, American Black Walnut &
Hard Maple

Sometimes interior designers must
feel as if they are creating a set for the
theater. Within a new speculative town
house in Baltimore, Maryland, **Rita St. Clair**
created the special effect of an Edwardian-
era house with the detailing of woodwork
found on a ship.

The house sits on the edge of Baltimore
Harbor in the Fells Point neighborhood,
where one can find many houses dating back
to the early 1700s and now listed on the
National Register of Historic Places. The
owner of the home, who owns and operates
a local contract furniture factory, suggested
that the expert cabinetmaker Edward Hough
work out of the factory to fabricate the
woodwork, which employees at the factory
then would finish.

"To re-create an Edwardian look and
texture required quality woods, cut in a
specific way and finished in an appropriate
manner," says St. Clair. "Grain was emphasized and matched, and burl veneers were
used to create textural variation."

The result is a set made for living as
well as dreaming.

CABINETRY: *David–Edward, Ltd. with Edward Hough*

*The entire living room is paneled
in a combination of American black
cherry and Honduras mahogany.
Incorporated in the paneling is
storage for television, photograph
albums, files, audio system and
other items. Display niches flank
the pair of leaded-glass doors that
open into the kitchen. The
approach to finishing the wood
was to first seal the wood so its
pores would be closed, then a
French polish was applied to
provide a slight sheen.*

Photography by Tim Fields

Under the American black cherry-paneled staircase are three arched openings, the doors of which have been painted with a trompe l'oeil illustration of memorabilia dear to the client's heart. The doors conceal a water heater, firewood storage and a coat closet. The cherrywood molding joins the entry to the baseboard, crown molding and other door openings for which cherry also is used.

SHAKER STYLE

American Black Cherry, Rock Maple &
Eastern White Pine

Sandra Nunnerley found the inspiration she needed for the total renovation of this Woodstock, Vermont, vacation home when she saw an authentic Shaker chest while touring the Winterthur Museum in Wilmington, Delaware. The simplicity of Shaker design, much of it executed in wood, suited the informality the clients wanted and also complemented the rustic mountain setting. Also, since Nunnerley has long believed in letting different elements and design periods complement each other, she was intrigued by the opportunity to mix Shaker furniture and architectural detailing with the clients' contemporary art collection.

Throughout every room, the designer remained true to her chosen theme by using hardwoods that the Shakers have traditionally used — pine, cherry and maple. Also, as is typical in Shaker homes, she used only local woods and craftsmen.

LEFT *A square grid of pine and glass was used in the entry to open up the space.*

BELOW *When the upstairs ceiling was opened up, decorative pine beams from an old farmhouse were installed.*

LEFT *The floors, doors, moldings and door casing are all fabricated in hard rock maple, as are the wainscoting and vanity in the bathroom.*

Photography by Grant Mudford

CUSTOM CABINETRY AND WAINSCOTING: **Skaskiw Case and Cabinet Company**
FANBACK CHAIR, REPRODUCED FROM A DESIGN BY HANS WEGNER:
Scandinavian Design
SHAKER FURNITURE: **Scott Jordan**

The wainscoting in the dining area surrounding the staircase is made of Eastern white pine. The fanback chair is a reproduction of the original Hans Wegner design.

The furniture was mainly made in American black cherry by Scott Jordan, who is noted for his construction of solid hardwood furniture in Shaker styles using time-honored techniques. All parts are joined with close-fitting mortise-and-tenon joints, either wedged or pegged. Flat panels are secured and stabilized with dovetail batons to discourage warping. The furniture is sealed and finished with several coats of clear penetrating oil, each coat being rubbed by hand. Finally, the piece is carefully polished with wax.

The dining chairs are made of rock maple because of its strength, with colorful seats woven in durable cotton canvas webbing. The round dining table is of American black cherry.

TUDOR TERRIFIC

Yellow Pine, English Pine & White Pine

What Dennis and Diana Hellman got when they purchased their fanciful romantic Tudor house was a number of elements not at all fanciful. Especially out of place in this Larchmont, New York, home was a dreary maid's room, which they did not need, and a cramped breakfast room and kitchen filled with fifties-style laminates, which they did not like. What they wanted was an open family room, eating area and kitchen that would echo and enhance the handcrafted character of their home. Enter the husband-and-wife design team, **Lucinda Wanner Stoll** and **Peter Ned Stoll.**

Their design is a richly layered collage of materials, patterns and textures organized into a structured framework that progresses from kitchen to family room to inglenook. The kitchen is the most horizontal and contained space, with the eight-foot-high ceiling brought even lower by a grid of heavy pine beams salvaged from a barn in Vermont. The ceiling in the more

TABLE, CHAIRS AND BANQUETTE: *fabricated by Peter Kramer*

ABOVE & OPPOSITE *In the kitchen area, the collage of materials, shapes and colors includes the floor, a pattern of squares, diamonds and planes in yellow pine and handmade saltillo tile. The cabinetry was custom-designed and executed in resawn English pine barn siding, its raised panel fronts milled with many details, cutouts and open shelves.*

LEFT *The inglenook has less texture than the kitchen, its floor being simple fourteen-inch-wide yellow pine planks with antique nails. The walls are a mixture of white pine paneling, windows and hand-carved banquette.*

Photography by John Herr

open family area incorporates the reclaimed beams as collar ties in one direction to open up the ceiling into a gable form. The inglenook is proportioned more vertically, emphasizing its tall pyramid ceiling. There the heavy beams have been replaced by clear white pine trim to accentuate the forms, including an array of tall windows overlooking Larchmont Harbor — fancies of a Tudor manor restored.

Viewing Yesterday Today

White Ash, White Oak & Purpleheart

Vishva Priya restructured this West Village residence in New York City's Old Amsterdam area, in what was once a meatpacking plant built on top of early-nineteenth-century houses, by incorporating wood throughout for the warmth especially necessary when one is dealing with ruins. These ruins included uncoursed walls of brick and stone. What they needed — beyond soap and water — was the touch of a softer, but also natural, material: wood.

"I used wood," he says, "for the requirement of closets, storage areas and display shelving, and I selected one wood primarily — white ash for the cabinetry and wall paneling — to anchor one strong presence throughout."

To emphasize particular functions, he used white oak for the floors and purpleheart for the stair treads. The important idea was to anchor everything that had been there before with one basic material — wood — for the necessities of today, and for the feeling of warmth and comfort, which always has been, and is, a necessity.

WOOD PANELING AND ALL CABINET WORK: *Valente Souza, Inc.*
WOOD SUPPLIER: *Rosenzweig Lumber Corporation*

ABOVE *To define function, Priya distinguished the stair treads using the dramatically hued purpleheart wood.*

RIGHT & OVERLEAF *The white ash paneling commences Priya's use of wood to create a touchable, living, earthy feeling that brings life to the previously dark interior. White ash is also used to frame the glass light fixture.*

Photography by Michael Moran

Cedar California Redwood Red Oc

White Oak B   Alder Walnut Rock Maple Eastern White Pine Englis

an Walnut Amaranth European Cherry Akatio White Birch Teak French Walnut

Western Red Cedar California Redwood Red Oak Lodgepole Pine Cedar Hondur

der Amaranth American Black Walnut Rock Maple Eastern White Pine English

an Cherry Akatio White Birch Teak Fre   White Ash Macassar Ebony

White Oak Butternut Red Alder American Black Walnut Rock Maple Eastern

an Walnut Amaranth European Cherry Akatio White Birch Teak French Walnut

Lodgepole Pine   Cedar   Honduras Mahogany   Eucalyptus Saligna   Radiata Pine   P

ine   Purpleheart   Pearwood   Eucalyptus   French Walnut   Whit   sar Ebo

hite Ash   Macassar Ebony   Red Oak   Douglas Fir   Redwood   Honduras Mahogany

Mahogany   Eucalyptus Saligna   Radiata Pine   White Oak   Butternut   Lodgepole Pin

Purpleheart   Pearwood   European Walnut   Amaranth   Pearwood   White Birch

d Oak   Lodgepole Pine   Cedar   Mahogany   Eucalyptus   Eastern White Pine   Red

ite Pine   English Pine   Purpleheart   White Birch   Teak   French Walnu

hite Ash   Macassar Ebony   Red Oak   Douglas Fir   Redwood   Eastern White Pine

LUSTROUS EXPOSURES

Pearwood, White Birch Plywood & Beech

When architect **Emanuela Frattini Magnusson** designed this second home in Paris for an American couple, her main consideration was to utilize the expansiveness of the loft-like space to accommodate their collection of contemporary paintings and sculpture. Many of the pieces are sizable, and all are so commanding that they require distance and space to be fully appreciated.

Her decision was to let the ceiling's existing wood beams remain visible and allow the perimeter walls, gypsum board that she painted white, to soar the full two-story height with a few individual rooms set like cubes within. The result is a constant interplay of large and small volumes which is exceedingly dramatic and made all the more immediate by the treatment of walls and cabinetry.

In the kitchen, white birch plywood has been given a hard, smooth finish of polyester lacquer in two tones of bright yellow. Although there is purposefully nothing purely decorative other than the art, the detailing of the woods, including dovetail joints and wood glides, provides a high degree of visual pleasure.

The unifying ambience of this spare but very appropriate approach makes a decidedly simple space extraordinarily rich.

CABINETRY BY: *Pierluigi Ghianda & Company*

White birch plywood, finished with polyester lacquer for a smooth, hard coating, defines the kitchen in Frattini Magnusson's cube-within-a-cube design for this Paris loft apartment. Swiss pearwood is used throughout for baseboards and also in the library cabinetry. The table, modified from the original design by Gianfranco Frattini, is of beech.

Photography by Mario Carrieri

THE DIFFERENCE IS IN THE DETAILS

Western Red Cedar

In the way an interior both looks and works, **Barry Brukoff** provides maximum effect through a minimal number of materials. Here there is only one that predominates, and that is wood.

After the John and Carolyn Collins home was destroyed in the 1991 fire in Oakland, California, he worked with them and their architect, **John Seals,** on its complete reconstruction and completely altered interior design. "The Collinses wanted the feeling of their original house but not a copy," says Brukoff. "The original house was all California redwood, but in order to not further deplete the old-growth redwoods, we used painted composition board on the exterior and Western red cedar for the interior."

RIGHT *When evening falls, concealed low-voltage lighting on top of the beams gives a glow to the cedar ceiling.*

Photography by Richard Barnes

The abundant use of the richly hued cedar led Brukoff to use brightly contrasting upholstery and powder-coated finishing on some other elements, as in the solarium, to keep the result from appearing too heavy.

Yet it is the way that cedar paneling was utilized that makes the real difference. Too often wood paneling is installed with rough edges that are then covered with another piece of wood to conceal the poor workmanship. Here, all boards are fitted flush to the end of each plane and mitered, cut at a forty-five-degree angle so that they wrap cleanly around each corner. The boards are also matched and cut in tongue-and-groove joints so they fit together seamlessly, fully capturing the rich beauty of wood's natural grain and color variations.

GENERAL CONTRACTOR: *Kaare Gjerde, Gjerde Construction Co.*
CUSTOM WOOD FURNITURE: *Julian Giuntoli*
KITCHEN CABINETRY: *Mueller Nicholls Co.*
CEDAR PANELING: *Delta Cedar (Canada) through Melrose Lumber Co.*
FRENCH DOORS: *Pittsburg Door Co.*

ABOVE *At the library's entry, the pocket doors were not sandblasted, as there was no need for privacy, and clear glass allows the spaces to flow together without visual interruption.*

RIGHT *Mitered corners and tongue-and-groove joints give the paneling a seamless look.*

ABOVE & OPPOSITE *The pocket doors between the kitchen and dining/living area are like shoji screens, their sandblasted glass allowing privacy when desired without cutting off the light. The dining table and buffet doors are fabricated of lacewood to make them distinct from the predominant cedar.*

SYSTEM FOR LIVING

European Cherry, Akatio, European Walnut, Pearwood & Amaranth

Everything that Milanese designer **Antonia Astori** creates stems from her personal interpretation of Le Corbusier's belief that cabinetry should be viewed not as separate from the architecture, but as part of it. In her modular systems manufactured by Driade since 1968, she has created a seemingly endless assortment of wood, laminate, glass and metal elements in various colors and finishes which enable customers to express their personal tastes as well as choose storage units that will be in harmony with their homes' architectural styles. To see how she would do that herself, a visit to a home designed by Astori reveals not only an architecturally harmonious use of her modular cabinetry, but of numerous pieces of her freestanding furniture, also produced by Driade.

OIKOS MODULAR FURNITURE AND SANS SOUCI COLLECTION:
Manufactured by Driade

LEFT *In the daughter's bedroom, the designer used the Eloise cabinet, which she designed as a major architectural statement itself. The cabinet is made of pear and amaranth (also known as purpleheart) with grids in rosewood and is part of the Sans Souci Collection.*

Photography by Aldo Ballo

ABOVE *In the living room, the designer combined her custom angular Wilhelm writing desk from her Sans Souci Collection with a bookcase composed of her Oikos modular container system. The desk is finished in European cherrywood and ebonized akatio wood. The bookcase is made of lacquered laminate panels.*

Astori custom-finished the shelving in this bedroom in European walnut with ebonized inlays to harmonize with the Franz Joseph canopy bed, from her Sans Souci Collection, which is made of European walnut and ebonized akatio wood with metallic connections in brass. In the foreground is her Alma Ditha vanity, also from the Sans Souci Collection.

RIGHT *Sisal flooring and Russian fossilstone combine with white birch to create an elegantly simplified palette of color and texture.*

Photography by Michael Ives

LIMITED PALETTE, LIMITLESS WARMTH

White Birch

One has come to expect a few but very strong strokes in the highly edited materials palettes **Rand Elliott** selects for each project, and here he has pared them down to primarily one. His use of select white birch, with a flat lacquer finish, for walls, ceilings and much of the furniture in this exclusive penthouse at Remington Park Racetrack in Oklahoma City, is as elegant as the thoroughbreds beyond ... yet so durable that they might as well race on in!

Designed for Ackerman Hood and McQueen, the park's advertising agency, the design was to provide a unique statement about the firm as well as accommodate up to thirty-five guests comfortably and unpretentiously. The white birch, illuminated from reflected daylight and incandescent sources, meticulously conceals all mechanical systems so that its own rich natural texture remains sveltely undisturbed. The result is a glow, sunup to sundown, with which any corporation would vie to be identified and in which any guest would surely feel at home.

GENERAL CONTRACTOR: **W.L. McNatt Contractors, Inc.**
CUSTOM MILLWORK AND COCKTAIL TABLES: **Troy Wesnidge**

Spatial flexibility was accomplished through the use of birch tables that split apart to become two smaller units. The armchairs, on casters, add further flexibility.

THE WELL-ORDERED STRUCTURE

Cherrywood & Purpleheart

In reconfiguring an apartment for Dr. Jay B. Adlersberg in a 1920s landmark building in New York City, **Margaret Helfand** and her associate **Marti Cowan** pulled functional elements, such as bookcases, audiovisual systems, desk and bed, away from the walls. This allows the original details of the walls, windows and doors to read in juxtaposition to these newly created elements. The result is profound visual excitement ... and profound order as well.

The expression of structure and materials is central to the design, as are the natural hues of those materials, cherrywood and purpleheart. These rosy and amethyst-colored woods are used for all primary horizontal surfaces of the custom-designed bookshelves and tabletops, which were constructed of solid planks of the two woods with exposed joints expressing their thickness. In addition, the cherrywood and purpleheart are juxtaposed throughout, creating colorful contrast and bringing the eye's attention to the details.

Millwork: **John Haggerty**

"Design is a marriage of order and structure," comments Margaret Helfand. *"Order is intangible, made of ideas. Structure is tangible, and made of materials. The programmatic elements of this project express the nature of the materials of which they are constructed. Wood is used for horizontal, tactile surfaces, expressing the capacity to span distances as a flat plane. In contrast, steel, in thin, bent planes, is efficient and elegant for vertical support."*

Photography by Paul Warchol

SENSUOUS VOLUMES

White Oak & American White Ash

It may seem ironic, but sometimes, even in the most minimalist interiors where the look of as few materials as possible is desired, two woods must be used to achieve the effect of one.

Architect **J. Frank Fitzgibbons** is ever involved with efficient, pared-down design. His goal is the creation of uncluttered environments so that the emphasis can instead be on serenity, which he views as "food for the soul."

To achieve that goal in this California residence, he wanted the unifying look that using just one kind of wood would provide, yet to do so required the use of two — white oak for the floors and white ash for the cabinetry. "If the same oak used for the flooring were used for cabinetry, its grain would

All floors are white oak, and all cabinets are American white ash, which, when finished with two coats of polyurethane, has the same color as the oak.

Photography by Toshi Yoshimi

FLOORING: **Bruce Hardwood Flooring**
CABINETRY: **Glendale Custom Cabinets**

*In the main living area, the
wood is juxtaposed primarily
with copper laminate, burnished
by hand with a wire brush.*

become more apparent and give it a reddish
cast that doesn't occur on the floor."

To provide a more exact color match,
he found that making the cabinetry not of
white oak but of white ash, with two coats of
polyurethane applied, was the answer —
one that allowed him to eliminate yet one
more stroke from this minimalist play of
light, volume and color.

ENLIGHTENED GEOMETRY

White Pine, Honduras Mahogany &
White Oak

Mexican architect ***Agustin Hernandez*** is always showing us how to appreciate space through the strong geometric shapes which pervade his designs. His immense circular windows draw our attention to the outdoors no matter what the weather. His massive rectangular coffee tables have a commanding presence regardless of what they have on top. His spiraling stairways suggest an exciting feeling of ascent, and his doors make us feel we are entering into a completely new and different dimension. Hernandez sees his mission as one of making us aware of our environment in an almost meditative way. And he succeeds.

RIGHT *The salute of a circular white oak base begins the launch up a spiral steel staircase and underscores Hernandez's belief that stairs are not just for circulating, but for symbolizing ascension as an almost metaphysical act.*

Photography by Tim Street-Porter

LEFT *An entry door of white pine, covered with a thin layer of aluminum which has been applied from the center outwards, gives those who enter the impression that they are passing through the sun.*

Photography courtesy of Agustin Hernandez

Dramatic circles rhythmically repeated along this living room's walls accentuate the rich tones of the Honduras mahogany, hand-rubbed with lacquer.

Photography by Tim Street-Porter

PLANES IN SPACE

Teak, French Walnut & White Ash

To a very great degree, these residences designed by **Robert D. Kleinschmidt** and **Donald D. Powell** reflect the concept of planes in space that was put into practice by their mentor, Ludwig Mies van der Rohe.

In one home, located in a Chicago high-rise building that Mies van der Rohe himself designed, their typically minimalist modernistic approach is carried out by planes of carefully selected, highly figured teak. The wood storage unit is deliberately kept at three-quarters of the room's height. The table is made of four individual cubes, each visually defined as a half-module of the building's planning grid. The leather desk top is raised just enough to visually separate it from the wood in order to make it, too, seem a plane in space.

RIGHT *Powell designed the table, too, of four individual cubes, each a half-module with a half-inch space between them. Made from the same tree as the storage unit, its grain pattern on top is diamond matched. The dark color of the rug, brown-black with a touch of purple in the dye, complements the honey-gold teak and adds a sense of solidity, making the coffee tables seem to float in space.*

Photography by Jon Miller, Hedrich-Blessing

ABOVE *On the other side of the storage unit is a carefully detailed desk designed by Powell, with its leather top raised three-eighths of an inch to visually separate it from the wood, further emphasizing the idea of planes in space. The teak desk chair, designed by Powell, is similar to the armless chair Mies van der Rohe designed in 1915, which was also of teak. The use of the same wood on all furnishings furthers a sense of unity, as does Powell's use of the same leather for desk top and custom letter tray and wastebasket.*

BELOW *By removing the wall that formerly divided the living room from the study and placing the storage unit there instead, the designers enabled light to flow above and below the two areas, furthering the sense of spatial richness.*

In another example of their work, a living room in an apartment in Naples, Florida, they used white ash for the louvered doors and for the ceiling slats, which assemble to create a cloud or plane. The doors and acoustical ceiling establish a theme of regionality even as the doors allow air to flow and the slatted ceiling absorbs sound.

WOOD FABRICATION: *Woodwork Corporation of America*
WOODWORK: *John Langenbacher Company, Inc*

White ash, used for the louvered doors and slatted acoustical ceiling, establishes a tropical feeling in this Florida residence, as does the rattan of the lounge chairs and chaise designed by Paul Kjørlholm in 1960. The straw cloth panels behind the sofa as well as the acoustical ceiling absorb sound and provide visual clarity in this play of planes in space.

Photography by Jim Hedrich, Hedrich-Blessing

Fun and Funky

Red Oak, American Black Cherry, American White Ash & Macassar Ebony

Oh, the many faces of wood. The ones used in this project by designer **Morlen Sinoway** — oak, cherry, white ash and ebony — could evoke visions of some sophisticated Transatlantic liner. But for this, his own loft space in Chicago, he used them in a manner that is ironic, humorous and ... well, come to think of it, highly sophisticated, too!

When Sinoway first saw the 1,500-square-foot space, it looked like a ship that had been hit by a torpedo. And, it didn't have plumbing. Creating everything from scratch, he carved out bedrooms, baths, laundry and storage, with a goal to have enough space left over for a spacious living/kitchen area that would provide enough dining space for soirées of six. Since this would definitely be the hub of activity in this home, he devoted the rest of his energies to making the kitchen reflect the casual — and

BELOW *In the bathroom a cherry vanity floats ten inches above the floor with details repeating the kitchen's circle motif. For extra size and depth, Morlen Sinoway used Kohler's half-round kitchen sink. Compressed particle board has been painted and then inset 3/16" within the frame of the pocket door to which he applied 3/4-inch-thick circles of the same painted material to heighten the dimensional look.*

Photography by Kevin Smith

ABOVE *A sculptural leg, designed by Sinoway, supports the counter and adds a whimsical touch to this creative loft space.*

Photography by Kevin Smith

fun — style of at least one of his dreams.

The result is really a collage: squiggly black-and-yellow laminate for the back-splash; American black cherry cabinetry, naturally patinated to a rich, dark honey, with a satin finish and topped with a navy laminate for the counter. Preferring to eat with his two feet on the ground rather than on barstools at a counter, Sinoway selected a highly textured American white ash for his undulating, table-height, dining surface,

supported by two sets of triple legs, satin-finished. One final touch or two: knobs of Macassar ebony ... a special, one-of-a-kind ringed counter leg designed by Sinoway and carved by George Pagels Company ... and, mission accomplished.

ABOVE *Inspired by the funkiness of the situation — a loft space in what had been a turn-of-the-century silk dry cleaning plant — Morlen Sinoway decided to go funky with his own design as well. As a living reminder of the loft's history, he preserved the existing floor, industrial-strength red oak that retained bits of green paint remaining even after numerous sandings, with a semi-gloss polyurethane finish. Also in keeping with the space's light industrial past, he made the kitchen lighting from scratch, rewiring found industrial lamps, boat hardware, copper and other industrial parts.*

Photography by Leslie Schwartz

CABINETS AND COUNTER: *Morlen Sinoway, fabricated by Bob Robinson Furniture*
COUNTER LEG WITH RINGS: *Morlen Sinoway, fabricated by George Pagels Company*

Unified Vision

White Oak & Red Alder

Why do some remodeled homes look like a hodgepodge, whereas others express a oneness that improves upon the original? Often, as exemplified in these two areas of a totally renovated house by The System Design's **Mark Warwick** and **Kim Hoffman**, the latter is a result of a decisive, limited palette of colors and materials carried throughout each room with the aim of establishing a cohesive unity.

In this project, the architects and designers used American white oak predominantly in their extensive custom-designed cabinetry and built-in and freestanding furniture. Today there is a harmonious flow from kitchen to master suite and to every room in between. One has no doubt that one strong vision shaped them all.

ABOVE *The custom-designed built-in eating area is fabricated from American white oak solids and veneers and suspended on a single steel pedestal embedded into the concrete slab underneath the wood flooring.*

Photography by Grey Crawford

ABOVE *The two cabinetry pieces in this master bathroom are fabricated from American white oak, which has a light stain, and red alder-wood solids, which have been painted with a black rubbed-through finish. The built-in cabinetry between the two sinks provides shelving above for easy access vides shelving above for easy access* *as well as drawers below. Since this bathroom had limited space and the design called for pedestal sinks, this area also provides space to store items below the shelves. Additionally, the framed mirrors of similar materials and finish are hinged to a custom-inset medicine cabinet for added storage.*

What formerly was a series of small isolated rooms did not work for the clients, who entertain often. The designers opened up the kitchen/living/dining area so that it now encompasses a large gourmet kitchen, expansive prep/eating counter and built-in kitchen eating area that comfortably seats eight. The rounded end of the kitchen counter was designed as a work space as well as an eating counter. The wood used is American white oak with an inlay of twenty-gauge stainless steel.

SIMPLY SUPERB

*American Black Cherry, Rock Maple &
White Ash*

Using wood allows **Clodagh** to fulfill several major tenets of her design philosophy — to use natural materials that are replenishable, artisan finishes that create a pre-eroded environment that is non-toxic and low-maintenance, and to create a look that only nature can improve.

TABLES, DISPLAY UNIT, BEDS AND PAVILIONS: **Clodagh Design Works**
WOOD SUPPLIER: **Rosenzweig Lumber Corporation**

BELOW *For a collector of miniature shoes, Clodagh designed this display grid so that each category could be appropriately displayed within. She used white ash for both the cabinet and the rolling dining table beneath, due to the relatively low price of ash and also its interesting markings, which she washed with a soft gray-green to pick up the wood's natural veining as well as provide a lightly antique look.*

Photography by Daniel Aubry

For clients in Aspen, Colorado, who entertain frequently, Clodagh designed a table that can seat fourteen guests comfortably but which also can easily be reduced in size for groups of six. Shaped slightly like a shield, the table is made of solid American black cherry with an asymmetrical aluminum center leaf that can be removed and hung on a wall bracket — becoming a stunning wall sculpture. The wood is finished with a nontoxic sealant. The base is aluminum. The edge of the table has a bow-like profile to celebrate the thickness of the material.

ABOVE & OPPOSITE *For a New York theatrical producer, Clodagh designed a room that can accommodate up to four houseguests and also serve as an office. White ash veneer was selected to create this double-decker installation. Two people can sleep in the loft beds — one on the sofa/bed, and one on the hideaway bed underneath. Work surfaces in ash are on either side of the ladder, with shelving for fax and copier behind the ladder. The*

third work surface is located at the window and is also of wood, this time almost totally obscured by a copper bronze wash which harmonizes with the window mullions.

Cedar   California Redwood   Re

White Oak   Butternut   Red Alder   Walnut   Rock Maple   Eastern White Pine   En

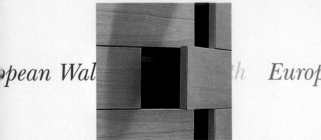

opean Wal   th   European Cherry   Akatio   White Birch   Teak   French Wa

Western Red Cedar   California Redwood   Red Oak   Lodgepole Pine   Cedar

Alder   Amaranth   American Black Walnut   Rock Maple   Eastern White Pine   Engl

opean Cherry   Akatio   White Birch   Teak   French Walnut   White Ash   Macassar Ebo

White Oak   Butternut   Red Alder   American Black   Maple   Eastern

opean Walnut   Amaranth   European Cherry   Akatio   White Birch   Teak   French Wa

Lodgepole Pine   Cedar   *Honduras Mahogany*   *Eucalyptus Saligna*   *Radiata Pine*

th Pine   *Purpleheart*   *Pearwood*   *Eucalyptus*   *Redwood*   *Red O*   *Pine*

White Ash   *Macassar Ebony*   *Red Oak*   *Douglas Fir*   **Redwood**   *Honduras Mahog*

s Mahogany   **Eucalyptus Saligna**   *Radiata Pine*   *White Oak*   *Butternut*   *Lodgepole*

ne   *Purpleheart*   *Pearwood*   *European Walnut*   *Amaranth*   *Pearwood*   *White Birch*

Red Oak   *Lodgepole Pine*   *Cedar*   *Mahogany*   **Eucalyptus**   *Eastern White Pine*   W

ite Pine   *English Pine*   *Purpleheart*   *Pearwood*   *White Birch*   *Teak*   **French Walnut**

White Ash   *Macassar Ebony*   **Red Oak**   *Douglas Fir*   *Redwood*   *Eastern White Pin*

Sky-High Comfort

Red Oak, Sugar Maple & American White Ash

It was for sophisticated elegance as well as the earthy, comfortable feeling provided by wood that led **Douglas Barnard** to use it extensively in these two residences situated in elegant New York City high-rise condominiums. Both were complete remodels.

WALL PANELS AND DOORS: *B+S and Lorch Woodworking*
FLOOR INSTALLATION AND FINISHING: *William Erbe and Sons*
WALL TREATMENT: *B+S and Lorch Woodworking*
CABINETRY: *Design Fabrication*

LEFT & ABOVE *For the entry hall, which opens into the dining room of this 7,000-square-foot private residence on New York's Park Avenue, Douglas Barnard used bird's-eye sugar maple panels finished with polished lacquer to enhance the unique bird's-eye flitches, in combination with antique waxed oak floors. Heavily textured wool fabric was applied to the wall and ceiling surfaces to help soften what otherwise would have been a space dominated by hard surfaces. The light wood panels were used to help the artificial skylight lighten what was once a dark interior room. The patterned red oak floor provides a serviceable surface, while its waxed treatment adds a sense of depth and tradition to the room.*

Photography by Paul Bielenberg

LEFT & BELOW *In the study of a Fifth Avenue penthouse apartment, designed for the chief executive of an international company for personal and business use, natural woods provide the ambience necessary for both. Individual sugar maple slats of varying width, depth and tone in the wall treatment provide a sense of security and stateliness as well as project a feeling of casual warmth. The use of the more formal lacquered and contrasting olive-tone burl of American white ash on the desk and expandable coffee tables establishes a needed sense of elegant stability, while allowing a less formal approach to the wall treatment than otherwise would have been necessary.*

Photography by Peter Vitale

CLEAN LINES, WARM FEELINGS

Pau Marfim

"Wood makes the atmosphere both clean and warm — the two qualities I am always after in my designs," says **Arthur de Mattos Casas**, and throughout his home in São Paulo are examples of his innovative design signature in one of his favorite materials, pau marfim, called ivory wood in Brazil.

"One of the most important aspects of selecting the kind of wood is to make sure it is replantable, that we aren't depleting a resource by using it," says the designer, who represents many other international furniture designers through his showroom, Casas Edições de Design. "Pau marfim, or ivory wood, meets this requirement, and I also prefer it for its brightness. It enhances the luminosity of a space."

LEFT & ABOVE *In the master bedroom, storage units are discreetly hidden.*

Photography by Tuca Reinés

Casas derives his inspiration from old furniture made by ancient artisans, then updates their designs to suit today's needs. To him, ivory wood is a classic material and, due to its dense surface, one of the finest materials one can use for the interior.

COUNTER: *Decorações Bom Lar Ltda.*
BAR/AUDIO UNIT: *Exímio Móveis e Decorações Ltda.*
STORAGE UNITS: *Decorações Bom Lar Ltda.*

LEFT & ABOVE *One continuous organically curved counter of pau marfim finished with a colorless impermeable wax integrates living and dining areas.*

THEMATIC VARIATIONS

*Red Oak, White Oak, Honduras
Mahogany, Brazilian Cherry & White Ash*

The work of **Gerard** and **Carlos Pascal** always expresses a dialogue between the many natural materials they use, and always there is wood in particularly sensual display.

"Wood is the friendliest material known to man," says Gerard. "It gives beauty and warmth to everything. It changes with time. It grows old with character. It even evokes the sense of smell."

RIGHT *The honey color and soft luster
of red oak used for this paneling
serves as a focal point in this otherwise black-and-white foyer.*

Photography by Victor Benitez

OPPOSITE *In this foyer and living room,
quartered white oak was selected for
the wall paneling so its light coloration
would provide contrast to the dark-green
granite floor. The oak is book-matched
to create a symmetrical pattern, and its
remarkable veining has been enhanced
by opening it with a steel brush.
The finish is a natural transparent,
semi-matte polyurethane lacquer.*

Photography by Eitan Feinholz

The Pascals' admiration for the richness of wood is given full display in this studio with Honduras mahogany ceiling and paneling. The floor is Brazilian cherry with white ash inlays.

Photography by Victor Benitez

SPECTACULAR PERSUASION

*Red Oak, White Alder, American White Ash,
White Oak & White Birch*

In rooms designed by **Erika Brunson**, wood wears many masks. Used extensively and variously — in one area she might specify latticework to create a room within a room; in another, dramatically overscaled shutters; in yet another, the detail of a carved lavatory bowl that looks like swagged fabric — it is one of the main ingredients in her always vivid expressions of luxurious living.

LEFT *In the powder room of a Middle Eastern villa, white alder has been carved to appear like draped fabric. The antique finish is accomplished by an application of bleach with a dry brush, then pickling.*

RIGHT *In a residence in Houston, Texas, a classical use of stained red oak applied to raised panel molding creates sensational boiserie and tremendous warmth.*

Photography by Billy Cunningham

RIGHT & BELOW *A combination of bleached American white ash, mirror and stone culminate in an intriguing wall unit for this European palace. The shutters are white oak, sandblasted and whitewashed without concealing the grain.*

The sleek, regular grain of American white ash has been stained a rich, strong hue for a grand home office in Europe.

The look of Brighton Pavilion inspired this romantic latticework structure of painted select white birch, a room-within-a-room in a Mediterranean palace.

Keeping the Magic

*American White Ash, Macassar Ebony &
Sycamore*

In his design of both interiors and furniture, **Adam Tihany** uses wood extensively. "I feel drawn to it," he says. "It represents a connection with nature's beauty and serves to remind us of the magic of ancient craftsmanship."

Not surprisingly, he has used an abundance of wood in these three residences otherwise quite removed from nature's mystery and majesty.

All are located in condominium buildings and situated high above Manhattan's bustling concrete boulevards. However the warm earthiness of wood — American white ash in one, sycamore in another and Macassar ebony in yet another — makes each of them feel firmly grounded in the best nature has to offer.

CABINETRY: *Fabricated by Capitol Cabinet*

RIGHT *Both straight and curved, these full-height veneered panels, made of American white ash and installed on concealed cleats, create a richly polished, elegant background.*

Photography by Mark Ross

RIGHT *Highly polished American white ash with black-lacquered details emphasizes nature's as well as the designer's artistry. Containers suspended from a wall unit contain all technical equipment.*

Photography by Andrew Bordwin

OPPOSITE *In this wood library, the color, stain and design of the Western plane tree wood, known in the United States as sycamore, reflect an informal approach in library design, suggesting a relaxed yet still-elegant lifestyle.*

Photography by Peter Paige

For a master bedroom, Adam Tihany designed the furniture out of a combination of American white ash burl and Macassar ebony to impart an Art Deco-style glamour.

Photography by Peter Paige

SUPERIMPOSITIONS

White Ash

It is as if **Juan Montoya** had placed one image on top of another, on top of yet another. In this New York high-rise apartment with an elevated view over Manhattan, he created an environment of utter starkness — white modernity at its purest — as if to make its inhabitants seem closer to the stars than the city at their feet. Then, as if to say that coldness is not the only thing we humans need in outer space, he added a wealth of richest white ash burl paneling, its olive cast deepened by a high-gloss, polyurethane finish, the earthy warmth of which is every bit as dominant as the galaxy of white. Finally, "to break the monotony still further" (as only Montoya would conceive of describing the juxtapositions already established), he framed the panels with bands of brass, thus superimposing an obviously manmade material over the natural burlwood.

The mix, seen altogether, is a tour de force as fascinating as the stardust beyond.

Since the edges of the veneer panels of the white ash burl are framed by brass bands, no seaming was necessary. The wood was sanded and finished several times to create the high-gloss, mirror-like finish.

Photography by Antoine Bootz

TOTAL BUILDOUT, ABSOLUTE KNOCKOUT

*Honduras Mahogany, Eastern White
Maple, Basswood, Carpathian Elm,
Lacewood & Aura Vera*

It was the perfect project for **Sheri Schlesinger**, who would just as soon start with nothing so that she has full leeway with the entire look. Above the concrete floors, this condominium was completely empty. She designed all interior architecture, installing floating walls for division that would still allow light to flow overhead between rooms. She did all the lighting, all backgrounds, all furnishings, all accessories, and some of the art. And to ensure that her preference for a clean, modern, but warm atmosphere could be achieved, she used a potpourri of exotic veneers — which were even more exotically dyed and painted. Says Schlesinger, "They cut the hardness out of contemporary."

RIGHT *In the living area, the game table is made of the highly patterned, aniline-dyed, crotch Honduras mahogany, a veneer cut from the point where two branches come together. The bar unit is made of lacewood, a silky oak from Australia.*

RIGHT *The hard, straight grain and rich color of the stained Eastern white maple, used with leather for a vanity chair, serves as counterpoint to the otherwise honey-beige palette of the powder room, including the vanity of blond aniline-dyed aura vera wood.*

Photography by Mary E. Nichols

BELOW *The designer selected aura vera, a blond type of sapele, for nightstands, powder vanity and screen. All aniline-dyed, the wood's striped figuring provides a complement to the extremely uniform grain of the basswood used for the painted shutters.*

BAR UNIT, POWDER ROOM VANITY AND NIGHTSTANDS: *Axis Furniture for The Bradbury Collection*
DINING CHAIRS: *K.A. Custom for The Bradbury Collection*
GAME TABLE: *Pace Collection*
POWDER ROOM VANITY CHAIR: *Totah Designs for The Bradbury Collection*
SCREEN, MASTER BEDROOM: *Philip Sicola Designs*
SHUTTERS, MASTER BEDROOM: *Accent Products*

The interesting, irregular grain and prominent growth-ring figure of the stained Carpathian elm used for the dining chairs works in contrast to the unpatterned clarity of the works of art.

TWO KITCHENS, TWO LOOKS

Padauk & Birch Plywood

There are as many styles as there are people, and there is a wood for every one. Exemplary proof are two kitchens remodeled by **John** and **Krista Everage** for two highly individual clients in two completely different environments.

Bright colors and new materials were the answer for the owner of this home, an Emmy Award-winning film animator. The cabinets are made of Fin Color Ply, a three-fourths-inch-thick industrial material composed of thin, multiple cross-banded Finland birch veneers. A phenolic film-faced product, Fin Color Ply has a surface film of cellulose impregnated with a phenolic resin. The result is a smooth, hygienic, cleanable, nontoxic surface that resists abrasion. Used in four different colors in this kitchen, Fin Color Ply makes the room look like one huge Mondrian painting.

Photography by Philip Thompson

CABINETRY: **Hartmark Cabinetry**
WOOD FINISHING AND DECORATIVE PAINTING: *Decorative Painting by Malcolm Moorman & Renée Tinnell*
PLYWOOD: **Finland Color Plywood Corporation**

In a 1920s Mediterranean-style California home, whose owners prefer traditional yet informal design, John and Krista Everage used richly hued and highly figured Burmese padauk, hand-rubbed with a clear wax, to impart a warm, earthy spirit throughout the custom kitchen cabinetry. Further setting off the wood's colorful grain is the black hand-forged iron hardware. Other wood enhancements include a rustic antique pine table used for the buffet and garlands of hand-painted vines encircling each of the stripped and refinished California redwood windows.

Cedar   California Redwood   Red

White Oak   Butternut   Red Alder   Walnut   Rock Maple   Eastern White Pine   Engl

bean Walnut   Amaranth   European Cherry   Akatio   White   French Waln

Western Red Cedar   California Redwood   Red Oak   Lodgepole Pine   Cedar   Hondu

Alder   Amaranth   American Black Walnut   Rock Maple   Eastern White Pine   Englis

bean Cherry   Akatio   White Birch   Teak   French Walnut   White Ash   Macassar Ebon

White Oak   Butte   der   American Black Walnut   Rock Maple   Eastern

bean Walnut   Amaranth   European Cherry   Akatio   White Birch   Teak   French Waln

URAL

Lodgepole Pine   Cedar   Honduras Mahogany   Eucalyptus Saligna   Radiata Pine

Pine   Purpleheart   Pearwood   Eucalyptus   Redwood   Re...epo... Pine   R

White Ash   Macassar Ebony   Red Oak   Douglas Fir   Redwood   Honduras Mahoga...

PRE

Mahogany   Eucalyptus Saligna   Radiata Pine   White Oak   Butternut   Lodgepole P...

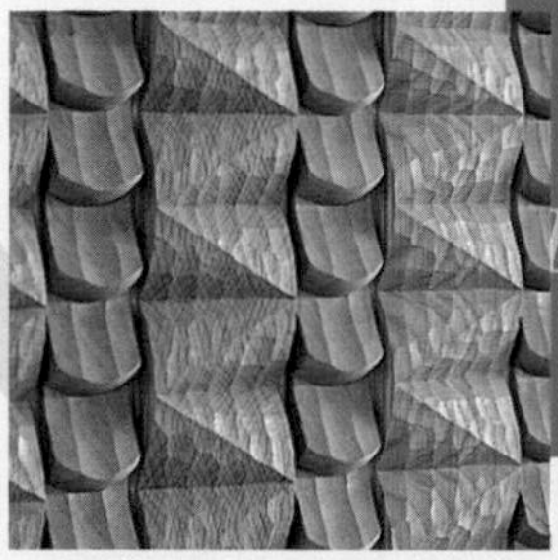

...ne   Purpleheart   ...   European Walnut   Amaranth   Honduras Mahogany   P...

Red Oak   Lodgepole Pine   Cedar   Mahogany   Eucalyptus   Eastern White Pine   Wh...

ORN

...te Pine   English Pine   Purpleheart   Pearwood   White Birch   Teak   French Walnut

White Ash   Macassar Ebony   Red Oak   Douglas Fir   Redwood   Eastern White Pine

LIVING TRADITION

Bamboo, Sitka Spruce & White Oak

In the work of Tokyo designer **Shigeru Uchida**, one senses an infinite sensitivity to past traditions in living artfully even as he reinterprets them for today's necessities. In these two projects, one a collapsible tearoom and the other, the Kazunari Furukawa residence in Nagoya, Japan, he addresses two aspects predominant in contemporary home life. In the first, he focuses on the desire for more flexible spaces; in the second, he responds to the wish to entertain without servants and in an increasingly informal manner. However, the materials and moods of these two projects remind one not only of present circumstances, but also of the elegant traditions of emperors and their samurai.

Working on the tearooms in collaboration with Uchida was lighting designer Harumi Fujimoto. Serving as chief assistants to Uchida in the design of the residence were **Kenichi Yokobori** of SDA Japan and **Yoshimi Tanaka** of Uchida's own firm, Studio 80.

TEAROOM FRAMES: *Furnicon International Co., Ltd.*
BAMBOO WORKMANSHIP: *Shinomiya Takezaikujo*

Shigeru Uchida comments on the three collapsible tearooms he designed for an exhibition organized by Sabie Cultural Institute and presented at Tobu Department Store in Tokyo:
"These tearooms are different from the ordinary ones rooted to the ground. These collapsible tearooms are more abstract, as they have no strong relationship with a specific location. They exist to draw the most possible feeling from the tea ceremony itself."
The identical cube-shaped tearooms, called by Uchida "Ji-an," "Gyo-an" and "So-an," are made of Sitka spruce frames and bamboo that has been woven differently for each one. Ji-an and Gyo-an emphasize the image of enclosure, whereas So-an (shown to the right of the others) has already established the separation of interior and exterior by the use of Japanese paper.

Photography by Nacasa & Partners, Inc.

Throughout the living/dining area of the Furukawa residence in Nagoya, Shigeru Uchida has used Nara oak, a kind of white oak found in Hokkaido, in all the cabinetry. Layers of thin paint and a clear lacquer help to create a sense of flow. He selected this wood because of its dense grain, fine surface and durability. Also, since its original color is light, it can be tinted any color. In this case, thin layers of finish were applied until the right color was realized.

The space is a solution to the contemporary style of living in which the host, in this case the president of an apparel company, and his wife can prepare the food and drinks within the same space without excusing themselves.

HOUSE AS VILLAGE

*American Black Cherry, European &
American White Ash, Hard Maple &
Tasmanian Oak*

The concept for this home, designed by architect **Stanley Tigerman** with interiors by architect **Margaret McCurry**, begins with the notion of a house as a collection of overlapping and changing functions. Each zone of activity is designed as a discrete building volume that interacts with the meandering "street" which unites the "village."

Floor finishes establish perimeters of overlapping volumes, and the pastel palette that differentiates the exterior volumes is echoed throughout the interior. Metallic paint, used on wood detailing throughout, refers to the metal roof as it relates to the forms it covers — forms and applications that are almost traditional, but which require a second reading.

WOODWORK: *Ron Parenti/Parenti & Raffaelli*

LEFT *The conceptual program for this project begins with the idea that a house is a collection of overlapping and changing functions, as shown by the way the parts of the "traditional" house are pulled away from each other, revealing the traditional home in all its parts.*

RIGHT *Quartered domestic cherrywood laid in a radial pattern forms the library's flooring. Plain sliced cherry veneer is used for the paneling as well as the game table, which has ebonized wood inlay patterns in the top. These variations of cuts of wood are a further expression of the village hierarchy, the importance of which, in this "village," is placed upon learning.*

Photography by Van Inwegen

Each individual room or "building volume" is further differentiated, one from another, by the use of different wood veneers to reinforce the idea or concept of separate buildings within a village. The dining room's floors are Tasmanian oak, the table is of European ash, and the cabinetry is of American white ash with natural finish incorporated with glass and metal. Aniline-dyed bird's-eye hard maple veneers were used in the kitchen and master bedroom because of their wide range of color possibilities — gray in the kitchen and celadon and natural in the bedroom.

FAR EASTERN CALM

Honduras Mahogany

ABOVE & RIGHT *Honduras Mahogany defines and enriches the entry, living/dining room and library of this apartment without sacrificing simplicity. The wood also delineates between these rooms: the ceiling was lowered in the entry, raised in the living room and raised still further in the library to visually create a succession of environments.*

Photography by Peter Paige

When Brennan Beer Gorman Monk/Interiors combined two separate apartments for a corporate client from Japan, Honduras mahogany was integral to a design that was to be rich in materials yet still reflect the simplicity associated with traditional Japanese design.

Expansive stretches of mahogany define the enlarged living areas' ceiling and baseboard moldings, wall finishes, flooring, radiator covers, and even the library's shoji-styled window screen and patterned transom. The way the wood is used also plays upon a Frank Lloyd Wright-inspired subtheme, as suggested by the client's authentic Wright doors which the designers installed at the entrance to the library.

The result has the sophistication appropriate for corporate entertainment, yet also the hospitable warmth one has come to expect from **Julia Monk**, the project's partner-in-charge, **William Whistler**, project designer, and **Michael Antonik,** project manager.

DINING TABLE: *Brennan Beer Monk/Interiors, fabricated by William Somerville Inc.*
GENERAL CONTRACTOR: *E.W. Howell Co., Inc.*

A transom compensates for the low height of the authentic Frank Lloyd Wright doors, and incorporates glass to complement a geometric pattern of Honduras mahogany paneling. The three-tiered stepped molding gives the library a sense of intimacy, and the window screen, also detailed in Honduras mahogany, allows for light to filter through evenly.

SERAPE BRIGHT

White Oak & American Black Walnut

Actress Rita Moreno wanted a warm, friendly, casual kitchen, and she got it. Designer **Mark Enos** used multicolored tiles that do not repeat, colorfully displayed baskets all askew, cabinet drawers randomly placed rather than marching in unison, and tin that was hammered by hand in Santa Fe and then, for an even more earthy look, bathed in acid.

Everything was to be festive and it is, but to create a counterpoint, Enos designed an equally earthy but far less brilliant island, letting the rest of the visual serenade circle around and overhead. The island is white oak with squares of American black walnut inset for the border. It was finished with clear polyurethane which, when dry, was hand-rubbed with steel wool and then waxed. The result is a virtually indestructible surface — and it maintains order amid all the purposeful disorder. ¡Olé!

CONTRACTOR: *Fort Hill Construction*

White oak was chosen for the island because of its warm color, durability and interesting grain patterning. The unusual style of the oval recessed door in the island was adapted from a picture of a yacht interior admired by the client, Rita Moreno.

Photography by Philip Thompson

Country Living, Urban Setting

Eastern White Pine, Douglas Fir, Red Oak, White Oak, Baltic Birch & American Black Walnut

This residence that has the appearance of a gracious "country home" is, in fact, an apartment in the middle of New York City. **Stephanie Stokes'** extensive assignment was to completely gut and refurbish everything — every square inch of the walls, cabinetry, wiring and air conditioning. The only aspect retained was the beautiful Eastern white pine paneling in the living room. Yet even that had to be restored — and it took five men four weeks to clean and polish it.

Of course, what sounds exhaustingly difficult to many is a delightful opportunity to this New York designer, who prefers, when possible, a complete renovation — it enables her to establish a unified look, as in this thoroughly country manor in an urban setting.

PANELING RESTORATION: *Eli Rios Restoration*
MANTELS: *William H. Jackson Company*
CABINETRY AND FLOORING: *Taconic Builders*

RIGHT & OPPOSITE *The living room's original Eastern white pine paneling was badly discolored after half a century of varnish and soot. After the removal of oils and waxes that coated the surface, the far lighter original color was revealed and then polished. Although newly manufactured, the base and crown moldings and doors are made of the same kind of pine. The floors are quarter-sawn red oak. The decorative trim and shells on the mantel were carved of no-knot Douglas fir, then antique-finished to match the paneling.*

Photography by John Hall

BELOW *Baltic birch plywood and solids were used in the library. First primed off-site, they were given a dark green glaze with a striated finish after installation.*

The cabinetry in the dressing room is Baltic birch plywood, painted on the exposed side to go with the room's other furnishings, but finished on the inside with clear lacquer for a fresh, clean feeling.

In the kitchen, the floor of plain-sawn white oak with American black walnut detailing provides a rich contrast to the painted Baltic birch solids and plywood. A medium brown stain was used for the entire floor after installation, making the inherently dark walnut appear almost black.

MODERN MEXICO IN NATIVE DRESS

Honduras Mahogany & Parota

As full of up-to-date amenities as are the spacious villas of Casa del Sol in Cancún, the aspect that most enriches the atmosphere is the generous use in every area of native materials handcrafted by Mexican artisans. In the case of wood, architects **Jaime and J. Manuel Gomez Vazquez** and interior designer **Marisabel Gomez de Morales** used hand-carved Honduras mahogany from Mexico for columns and beams and open-weave lattice-work made of parota wood to embrace doors and windows.

WOOD: *Internacional Maderera*
WOOD CARVING: *Arte y Madera*

LEFT & OPPOSITE *Open-weave lattice-work made of parota wood, native to Mexico and of lasting endurance in humid weather, is used extensively in decorative detailing and creates an exquisite frame for views of the Caribbean. The tabletop is mahogany.*

Photography by Scott McDonald, Hedrich-Blessing

The height and strength of Honduras mahogany trees from Mexico, cut into beams and hand-carved by local artisans, dramatically embellish the high, sloped ceilings and make entries majestic.

Remembering the '40s

American Black Cherry

It was an ironic about-face. Usually inhabitants of New York City's spacious loft spaces, typically located in old industrial buildings downtown, try to emulate the sophistication of homes uptown. Yet in this case, **Mark Zeff** was asked to completely reconstruct Nathaniel Kramer's uptown Park Avenue apartment to make it feel like a loft with a 1940s feeling. The dominant material used to recall that period was cherrywood, which he used throughout in his design of cabinetry, paneling, screens, dining table base, the seats of the dining chairs, and the bed.

American black cherry became the dominant material in the study, television, dining room and bedroom. Zeff admires cherry's unusual grain, which accepts stain well; its ability to age well, with its color deepening to an even richer hue; and also natural cherrywood's relaxed feeling. His simplified loft-like design not only gives the wood prominence, but also allows the rooms to flow.

Photography by Michael Mundy

SENSE OF HAWAII

Acacia Koa, Teak, Western Red Cedar,
Douglas Fir & Lodgepole Pine

Geographic location and local culture are always key elements in interiors by **Cheryl Rowley**, who, rather than simulating places where one isn't, believes in emphasizing a sense of the place where one is — especially when that place is Maui. Here, on five acres of rolling countryside on Haleakala Crater's northern slope, she selected a number of woods, predominantly acacia koa, teak, lodgepole pine and bamboo, to emphasize the rustic feeling of this part of the island. The architect for this 6,000-square-foot residence with guest house was **Hugh Farrington**.

FLOORING: *M+D Flooring*
CABINETRY: *Frank Jones*
LODGEPOLE PINE INSTALLATION: *Joe Hartley*

LEFT & OPPOSITE *Long before one enters the home itself, stained Douglas fir siding and painted Douglas fir trellis and woodwork, joined by numerous groupings of teak furniture for conversation and relaxation, create a sense of relaxed informality.*

BELOW *To lighten the effect of the kitchen's expansive use of richly hued acacia koa cabinetry and cedar beams, Rowley lacquered the Douglas fir ceiling decking white. The lacquer also protects against humidity.*

Photography by Steven Minkowski

Rowley depended to a great extent on wood to establish the country feeling in this part of Maui. Floors and cabinetry are of acacia koa, mantels and ceilings are Western red cedar, and furnishings are acacia koa, teak, yellow pine and Lodgepole pine. In addition, the wall of lava rock surrounding the fireplace in the main living room provides an exclamation point of local flavor, as do a number of handcrafted works, such as the breadfruit-pattern quilt in the dining room and another Hawaiian-style quilt in the bedroom. There is also an extensive collection of Hawaiian calabashes, framed tapa cloths and contemporary Hawaiian art. The waterwheel over the fireplace is Japanese.

NATURAL EVOLUTION

European White Birch, American White Ash, Honduras Mahogany, Japanese Maple & Rock Maple

Time and again during the development of modernism in California, the response to the clement weather has been to create indoor/outdoor environments, and this often has led to a feeling similar to that of a Japanese garden house. After all, that type of traditional house was itself a response to Japan's own similar Pacific environment. To architect **Steven Ehrlich**, the theme of this home derived not from importing an admired style and plunking it down out of context. Instead, the home evolved naturally from the site itself — an ample canyon in Southern California, defined by three gently sloping hills — and a natural extension of that evolution was that no tone could be more appropriate than the one established centuries earlier on the other side of the ocean.

The architectural concept was enhanced by interior designer **Luis Ortega's** selections for furnishings.

CABINETRY: *Steve Miller/Miller Woodworking*

ABOVE *The entry/living room cabinets, envisioned as giant glowing lanterns, are built out of Honduras mahogany and European white birch. Besides housing the entertainment center, the cabinets provide ample room to display the owner's extensive pottery collection.*

Photography by Tom Bonner

LEFT *Honduras mahogany-framed sliding doors graciously open all rooms onto the entry garden courtyard. The horizontal design of the mahogany banding is carried throughout the house in windows, cabinets and soffits and interior doors. The Japanese mood set in the entry garden also is reflected in the furnishings, as in this custom dining table made of Japanese maple, ebony and copper.*

ABOVE *The kitchen is generously detailed in rock maple, with six-inch-wide maple planks on the floor, cabinets of maple with a horizontal grain, and quarter-sawn bird's-eye maple on the central island.*

LEFT *Quarter-sawn American white ash paneling covers all wall surfaces of the powder room. The ash is comb grain, a quality of rift veneer with exceptionally straight grain and closely spaced growth increments, and conveys a feeling of serenity. The inset niches are covered in gold leaf.*

HERITAGE HONORED

*White Oak, American Black Cherry,
California Redwood & Teak*

What once was a cold, contemporary house lacking personal scale has been turned into such a congenial home, expressing so naturally the Mexican heritage of its owners, Frank and Alia Herrera, that today it feels as if it had been designed for them when it was first built. The transformation of this home in San Antonio, Texas, was due to the thorough and detailed direction of Ford, Powell & Carson's **John Gutzler**, who emphasized natural materials to reinforce the owners' collection of art and artifacts from Mexico. Included is a wealth of custom-designed, handmade and hand-carved furniture of American black cherry and white oak which works together with hand-worked stone, metal, tile, leather and fabrics to provide a sense of joy and a delightful interplay of visual accents.

RIGHT *The vertical face and horizontal shelves of a display cabinet in the living area are white oak with a light stain, while the back panels are American black cherry with a light stain. Conversion varnish finish was applied for durability. The cabinet was custom-designed by Ford, Powell & Carson and made by Alan Reams.*

Photography by Hickey-Robertson

ABOVE *The circular entry table is composed of a solid cherry bullnose edge with a cherry veneer top, white oak apron, pedestal and legs, which are separated by carved solid cherry spheres and balls.*

MILLWORK AND CABINETRY: *Ford, Powell & Carson, fabricated by A. Reams*
HAND-CARVED WOOD AND HAMMERED COPPER DETAILING: *Denise Kocourek*
ARMCHAIRS: *Summit Furniture, Inc.*
HANDCRAFTED SCREEN AND WOOD FEET ON SOFAS AND CHAIRS: *Alan Reams*
UPHOLSTERY: *Boggs & Oehler*

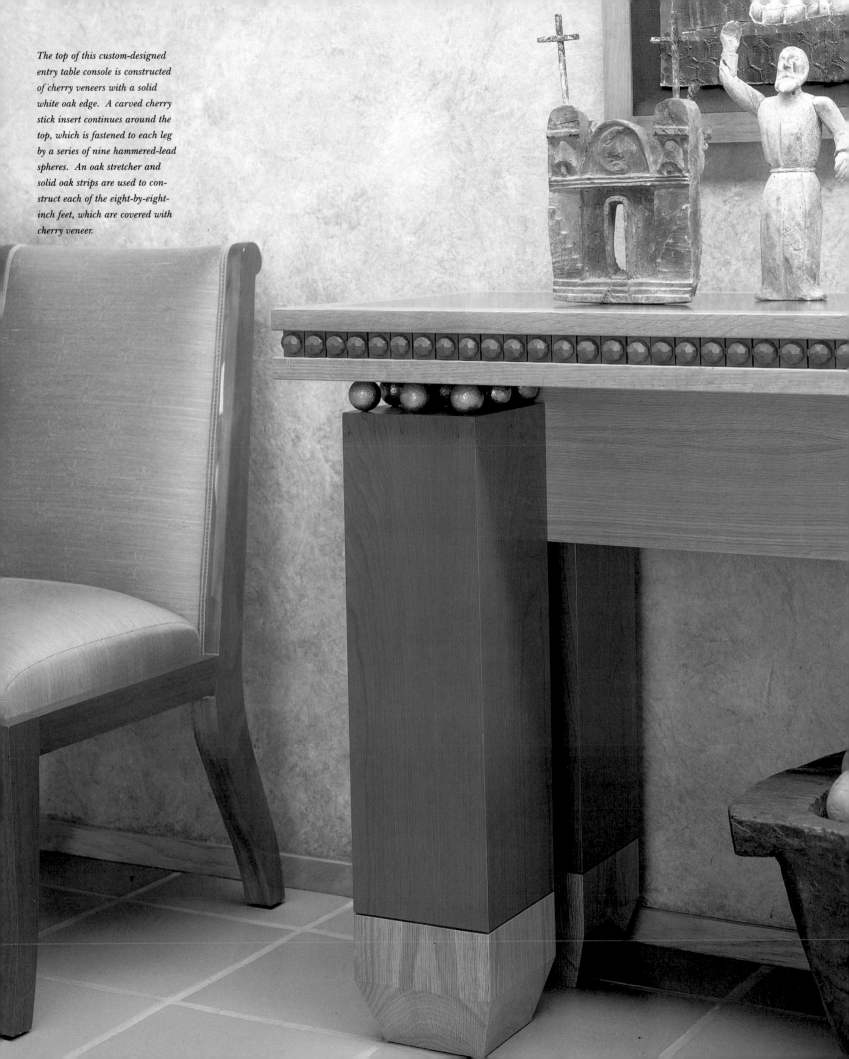

The top of this custom-designed entry table console is constructed of cherry veneers with a solid white oak edge. A carved cherry stick insert continues around the top, which is fastened to each leg by a series of nine hammered-lead spheres. An oak stretcher and solid oak strips are used to construct each of the eight-by-eight-inch feet, which are covered with cherry veneer.

ABOVE *This detail of the custom-designed chairs and sofas shows how the legs repeat the massive scale of the end tables and also continue the interplay of the two woods. The dense oak carving creates an interesting shadow effect that is softened by the American black cherry legs and bands.*

BELOW & OPPOSITE *The dining table, which divides into two for flexibility, is composed of a solid oak edge and cherry veneers over a slab of torsion box construction. The cherry veneers were divided into four panels, quarter-turned to create a pattern on top, then separated by a one-eighth-inch cherry strip to relieve the matching pattern of the grain. A one-eighth-inch strip of Gabon ebony was used to separate and accent the cherry veneer top and oak edge joint. A carved sphere pattern in cherry was used around the table. The cabinet's carved panels by Denise Kocourek, made of hand-carved and chiselled oak sticks separated by cherry sticks, create a rich visual interplay of shadows and forms.*

BELOW *Ford, Powell & Carson, also responsible for the landscaping, employed a series of four-by-six-inch California redwood timbers that were notched and pinned with half-inch redwood dowels to break up the space and reinforce the natural materials of the planting. The trellis is stained to match the teak armchairs.*

Wood accents, such as the wood screen and planter base in the living room, work with the other natural materials to provide an inviting sense of warmth and touch. The planter base and screen were both custom-designed by Ford, Powell & Carson and handcrafted by Alan Reams. Each thin blade of solid cherry is first planed, then sanded to minimum thickness before being woven into an exact form. The hinges are made of solid wood.

Chapter 6 WATERFRONT HAVENS

Cedar California Redwood Red Oak

e Oak Butternut Red Alder Walnut Rock Maple Eastern White Pine English P

Valnut Amaranth European Cherry Akatio White Birch Teak French Walnut V

ern Red Cedar edwood Red Oak Lodgepole Pine Cedar Honduras M

Amaranth American Black Walnut Rock Maple Eastern White Pine English Pine

Cherry Akatio White Birch Teak French Walnut White ar Ebony R

e Oak Butternut Red Alder American Bla Walnut Rock Ma Eastern White

lnut Amaranth European Cherry Akatio White Birch Teak French Walnut V

Lodgepole Pine   Cedar   **Honduras Mahogany**   *Eucalyptus Saligna*   *Radiata Pine*   *Purple*

Purpleheart   Pearwood   *Eucalyptus*   *Redwood*   *Red Oak*   Lo   *Red Oa*

e Ash   *Macassar Ebony*   *Red Oak*   *Douglas Fir*   **Redwood**   *Honduras Mahogany*

gany   **Eucalyptus Saligna**   *Radiata Pine*   White Oak   Butternut   Lodgepole Pine

urpleheart   *Pearwood*   *European Walnut*   *Amaranth*   *Honduras Mahog*   *Pearl*

Oak   *Lodgepole Pine*   *Cedar*   *Mahogany*   **Eucalyptus**   *Eastern White Pine*   *White Bi*

English Pine   *Purpleheart*   *Pearwood*   *White Birch*   *Teak*   **French Walnut**   *Maca*

Ash   *Macassar Ebony*   **Red Oak**   *Douglas Fir*   *Redwood*   *Eastern White Pine*   *Rad*

LIVING LIGHTLY ON THE LAND

Yellow Cedar, Red Oak & Douglas Fir

Nestled within a meadow on a rugged coast facing the Pacific Ocean, this home designed by **Bruce** and **Susan K. Burdick** for their own weekend retreat pays homage to the rigorous simplicity of its site. Rather than overload it with the highly technical industrial design discipline they bring to corporate, museum and retail clients worldwide, the technology integrated with the natural materials here is in the form of steel surfaces and off-the-shelf elements purchased at a local hardware store.

The mostly yellow cedar, barn-like home is located within Sea Ranch, conceptualized in 1965 by Larry Halprin, Charles Moore, William Turnbull and Joseph Esherick as a 4,000-acre development where structures, rather than serving as architectural statements, would sit lightly on the land. As the Burdicks' consistent goal has been to develop new forms which transcend

GENERAL CONTRACTOR: *Matheny Construction*
CUSTOM WOODWORK: *Sea Ranch Cabinets/Bob Little*
CEDAR SIDING: *Healdsburg Lumber*

LEFT *Built-in seating faces the modern black steel Danish wood stove. The dark stain of the floors, four-inch-wide red oak planks stained "red mahogany," provides contrast to the cream-colored painted walls and white trim. The natural, unfinished wood of the exposed Douglas fir rafters with yellow cedar roof decking and ridge beam emphasize the high, peaked ceiling. The walnut stool by Charles and Ray Eames serves as a reminder of the years Bruce Burdick spent in the Eames office.*

LEFT, ABOVE & OPPOSITE *A clear view from the entry breezeway through to the deck takes full advantage of the Sea Ranch clustering plan which enables all houses to have structure-free views. Since there are no fences allowed either, the perception is that one's lot extends endlessly over the meadow and toward the sea. Within this tranquil setting, the Burdicks designed a barn-like house with a symmetrically peaked roof and vertical yellow cedar siding with a natural finish. Industrial window sashing with powder-coated black paint finish begins the various expressions of the designers' interest in more technically inclined design references.*

Photography by Susan Lee Burdick

fashion, giving their work a timeless, quality-based, modern feeling, it was this informal covenant, that residents should build in harmony with the environment, that drew these San Francisco-based principals of The Burdick Group to a place so different from the humming urban context of their professional lives.

ABOVE *On the second story, the ridge beam is left exposed, but the rafters and clear yellow cedar ceiling are painted white to match the rest of the trim.*

ABOVE *Ready for an afternoon meal, the clear yellow cedar deck beckons.*

OPPOSITE *The designers' own Spring Table, with a Honduras mahogany top, manufactured by Herman Miller, is used as the dining table, surrounded by classic Prague chairs in natural cane. Yellow aniline-dye casework encloses the open kitchen beyond.*

FACING THE ELEMENTS

Redwood, Teak & Honduras Mahogany

When **Theodore M. Ceraldi** was asked to design this extended-family home on the Hudson River, he knew the materials would need to withstand as wide a range of weathers and temperatures as most ships at sea. He decided to use wood much as it is used in nautical design specifications, paying greatest heed on the exterior to those that are weather-resistant.

The home may look large, and it is, yet it serves many purposes, too — privacy for a professional office and parking for clients, entry gallery for art, private and common family entertainment and living areas, bedrooms for the owners, their children, their children's children, and domestic help. Still, the entire vocabulary of the architecture and the entire use of wood are derived from the geographical setting, a wide flat plane contained by steep cliffs on the west and rolling hills on the east. Vertical basaltic towers play against a pacific expanse of water, wide

Because the house is predominantly brick and limestone, the use of wood, primarily redwood on the exterior, becomes an important design element, on display at all times as a contrast against the masonry mass. The result is a question of balance. Exterior railings are of steel with a teak handrail, for teak has a natural oil that allows the wood to weather in a damp environment with minimum maintenance.

Photography by Brad Hess

GENERAL CONSTRUCTION: *Martelli Associates*
CALIFORNIA REDWOOD AND HONDURAS MAHOGANY: *Condon Lumber Co.*
WINDOWS: *Duratherm Window Corporation*
STRAIGHT STAIR: *Joseph Brandi*
SPIRAL STAIR, CARPENTRY AND RAILING: *Joseph Brandi*
SPIRAL STAIR, STAIRBODY: *Duvinage*

enough to be called a sea, or *zee*, by the early Dutch settlers. The concept of the house is a series of flat planes stepping down to to the river and vertical masonry piers and columns pinning and piercing the planes to the slope.

Divided into three pavilions interconnected by walks, a bridge and gardens, the design solution involved wood from the start as the horizontal elements, or planes, of the house. Wood is also used for the rails, doors, windows and trim. The roof planes and vents are trimmed with California redwood, chosen for dimensional stability, consistency of grain and color, and resistance to rot. Exterior railings are of steel with a teak handrail, for teak has a natural oil which allows the wood to weather and hold up to the damp river shore environment with minimum maintenance. The windows are made of teak on the exterior and Honduras mahogany on the interior. Mahogany is also used for the interior's doors, woodwork and interior stairs.

"The trick," says Ceraldi, "is to create a dichotomy between design elements so that one is not more important than the other. Every element is important and every material must be honestly presented. Architecture abhors a lie."

RIGHT & ABOVE *The two Honduras mahogany handrails were hand-carved and/or shaped before installation by master carpenter Joseph Brandi, who was coaxed out of retirement to make these two stairs.*

The interior trim is of Honduras mahogany as well as the doors, woodwork and interior stairs. Honduras mahogany was used exclusively because of its hardness, open grain and golden brown color. It is one of the world's finest cabinet and paneling woods. The finish of a low-luster varnish was applied after hand-sanding all railings and trim.

CARIBBEAN RETREAT

Red Cedar, White Pine, Honduras Mahogany & Greenheart

There is so little of anything on the island of Mustique and so few people to build what is there that the local contractors' familiarity with certain woods can be the best reason for choosing them. Thus, Toronto-based architect **A. J. Diamond** selected red cedar shingles that are endgrain "blue ribbon" premium-quality, Honduras mahogany, white pine and greenheart. Save that they all had to be imported, it was as simple as that.

Of course, simplicity in all things *is* Mustique. Diamond even named his home there "Simplicity." And the very purpose of his home's design was to disturb the natural landscape as little as possible. Its five separate pavilions were created to take advantage of the prevailing winds ... otherwise, they were scarcely to be noticed at all.

CEDAR: *Anglo American Cedar Products Ltd.*

ABOVE & RIGHT *Pitched shingle roofs of endgrain "blue ribbon" premier-quality red cedar are ventilated for cooling, while the flat greenheart batten roofs await vines to wind their way across. Also ready to welcome the breeze are the treated and painted Honduras mahogany louvered doors. The cedar was imported from British Columbia, the mahogany and greenheart from Guyana.*

RIGHT *Custom-made sliding glazed doors of white pine provide all the environmental control needed between this deck and eave.*

Photography by Tim Griffith

ABOVE & RIGHT *The roofs are made of endgrain, premier-quality red cedar, while the interior tray ceilings are white pine, and the exposed ceilings over the verandas are greenheart. All have been painted. A space between the roof and ceiling permits further ventilation. The wood itself, whether as shingles or tongue-and-groove boarding, also insulates.*

ECHOES OF A LUSH LAGOON

California Redwood, Carpathian Elm, Anegré, French Walnut, American Black Walnut & Incienso

The rooms of Christopher Hemmeter's Villa Kaikoo, whether those inside the expansive residence or the many outside which are open to the breeze but protected from the sun, echo the spirit if not the form of the site's lushly planted hillside overlooking Honolulu. With architecture by **Hemmeter Design Group** and interiors by the late **Steve Chase** and **R. Randall Patton**, the selection of woods and their carefully executed finishing, often completed on-site, reflect the abundance of the natural setting and the collections within.

WOOD CEILING CONSTRUCTION: *Kaya Builders*
FLOORING: *Yost/Flagship Flooring*
CUSTOM CASEWORK: *Schultz Custom Cabinets*

RIGHT *This exterior family lounge/living space is a peninsula set in a shallow, reflecting body of water. All soffits are clad in tongue-and-groove one-by-three-inch planks of solid weather-resistant California redwood that has been stained with a semi-transparent, bone/ivory pigment. The upper ceiling with stepped molding forms a grid with inset panels of acid-etched copper.*

Photography by Mary E. Nichols

LEFT *The selection and detailing of the woods for paneling, floors, desk and credenza in the estate's private office were inspired by Christopher Hemmeter's collection of European art, antiques and accessories, as well as the antique leather and warm gold-leaf finishes of the antique chairs. The effect is that of an antique writing desk in some hallowed library of yesteryear but without overdoing it — after all, the time is now and the conveniences could not be more up-to-date. Carpathian elm burl with ebonized and black lacquer accents refers to classical images and historical motifs. Panel frames, borders and moldings are of anegré, the name in the Ivory Coast for aningeria. The wood floor with Absolute Black granite inserts uses multiple hand-selected exotic woods including French walnut, the darker American black walnut and incienso. Ceiling moldings of similar wood veneers and solids were site-finished and -fabricated.*

BRINGING THE WAVES INSIDE

Douglas Fir, California Redwood, Teak &
Sugar Maple

The aesthetic temptation of the ocean-front location of Marty and Julie Safran's home in Laguna Beach, California, was too great to ignore. So architect **Gary Whitfield** softened his design's hard angle planes with so many curving forms inspired by the waves themselves that it looks as if their ebb and flow occurs not on the beach but inside every room.

GENERAL CONTRACTOR: *Bruce Scherer*
WALL UNIT, DINING ROOM: *NBI, Inc.*

RIGHT *The wave theme continues in the guest bedroom with the picket fence made of selected construction-grade California redwood applied to the ocean-blue wall. The feeling is that of sleeping underwater.*

RIGHT *In the dining room, medium-density fiberboard is used as a design element in the shaped soffit above the French doors, concealing the window treatment, as well as in the custom wall-mounted buffet of bird's-eye sugar maple veneer with an alcohol-dye finish. This particular finish allows the use of color to enhance the natural grain of the wood.*

Photography by Christopher Covey

The wave theme commences at the entry, with the curving form of the white picket fence and board-and-batten siding reminscent of the beach cottages found elsewhere in the neighborhood. The curving wood fence is made of Douglas fir. The board-and-batten siding is California redwood painted to blend with the character of the neighborhood. The front door is teak with a stainless steel porthole.

ROCKY MOUNTAIN MEDLEY

Lodgepole Pine & Radiata Pine

To design a home that has the strength of a log house yet the softness of the most comfortably aged country home in Europe is remarkable. Yet this is not the first time that ***Joseph Minton*** of Fort Worth, Texas, has done so for his clientele with second homes in the Rocky Mountains.

In this particular case, the project was a large log house on the Taylor River in Colorado, built almost entirely of wood. Structural lodgepole pine was used for interior and exterior walls and structural beamwork as well. The ceiling decking is radiata pine with knots, stained translucent blue. Upstairs the floors are planks of clear radiata pine. It is all natural wood — but that does not begin to describe the lived-in feeling Minton has achieved through the use of country antiques from France and England and hues so translucent that they seem to appear and disappear with the changing light.

RIGHT   *To further blend the newly placed wood with everything within, Joseph Minton had all the fabrics dyed the color of tea prior to printing. The resulting yellowish-brown harmonizes with the pine — the final expert touch that makes this home look as if it has been nestled along Taylor River for a long, long time.*

BELOW LEFT & RIGHT   *One brilliant stroke was Joseph Minton's choice of staining the ceiling deck a translucent blue, providing relief from the predominant hue of the natural pine and also bringing inside the feeling of sky in the way so familiar with country cottages in Europe. Using the blue overhead is particularly appropriate, as Minton left the site during construction to shop in Europe, bringing back a treasure-trove of rustic antiques and accessories such as pots and farm tools from the French and English countrysides.*

Photography by Hal Lott

G L O S S A R Y

Wood Types
A Glossary of the Woods Shown in This Book

Major Source:
Wood Handbook: Wood as an Engineering Material
United States Department of Agriculture
Forest Service
Agriculture Handbook 72
Prepared by the National Forest Products Laboratory

For woods not included in this glossary, please refer to the Wood Handbook, or telephone the National Forest Products Laboratory, Publications Department, at (608) 231-9200.

Acacia Koa (see Koa)

Akatio *(Gambeya africana)* Not Anegré, but closely related. Heartwood is whitish when first felled, then turns a pink-buff to an olive-yellow and finally a yellowish-brown, and is not demarcated from the sapwood. Texture is fine to medium, grain is straight to occasionally interlocked, luster is rather low. Wood contains a pale-brown gum.

Alaska-Cedar *(Chamaecyparis nootkatensis)* Also known as yellow cedar, Alaska-cedar has bright, clear yellow heartwood. The sapwood is narrow, white to yellowish, and hardly distinguishable from the heartwood. Fine-textured and generally straight-grained. Moderately heavy, moderately strong and stiff, moderately hard, and moderately high in resistance to shock. Shrinks little in drying, stable in use after seasoning, and the heartwood is very resistant to decay. Used for interior finish, furniture and cabinetwork.

Amaranth *(Peltogyne)* Amaranth as well as purpleheart are common names for the various species of this wood primarily from the north middle part of the Brazilian Amazon region, but also from Mexico and Central America. When freshly cut, the heartwood is brown but turns a deep purple upon exposure. Medium to fine texture. Usually straight grain. Strong and heavy. Air-drying is easy to moderately difficult. Moderately difficult to work with either hand or machine tools and dulls cutters rather quickly. The wood does turn smoothly, however, is easy to glue and takes finishes well. The heartwood is rated as highly durable in resistance to attack by decay fungi and very resistant to dry-wood termites. Extremely resistant to impregnation with preservative oils. Due to its unusual color, it is used in turnery, marquetry, cabinets, fine furniture, parquet flooring and many specialty items.

Amboyna *(Pterocarpus)* (see Padauk) A highly figured East Indian padauk.

American Black Cherry (see Cherry)

American Black Walnut (see Walnut)

American Red Alder (see Red Alder)

American White Ash (see Ash)

American White Birch (see Birch)

Anegré (see Aningeria)

Aningeria *(Aningeria)* A blond wood with a slightly pinkish tint. Similar in weight to African mahogany. Lustrous, fine and even in texture. Most often straight-grained, but sometimes the grain is wavy. Slices well into thin veneer, in which form it is most often used, its uniform texture accepting finishes simulating more decorative woods.

Ash Important species of ash are white ash *(Fraxinus americana)*, green ash *(F. pennsylvanica)*, blue ash *(F. quadrangulata)*, black ash *(F. nigra)*, pumpkin ash *(F. profunda)* and Oregon ash *(F. latifolia)*. Commercial white ash is a group of species that consists mostly of white ash and green ash, although blue ash is also included. Heartwood of commercial white ash is brown; the sapwood is light-colored or nearly white. Second-growth commercial white ash is heavy, strong, hard, stiff and has a high resistance to shock. Ash wood of lighter weight, including black ash, is sold as cabinet ash and is suitable for furniture. Some ash is cut into veneer for furniture and paneling.

Aura Vera (see Sapele) A blond sapele.

Baltic Birch (see Birch)

Bamboo *(species of some 45 genera)* Semitropical or tropical grasses which often resemble trees with woody stems that grow at times to more than one hundred feet in height. Sometimes confused with rattans, a type of palm. Used in light construction and furniture.

Basswood *(Tilia)* In commercial usage, "white basswood" is used to specify the white wood or sapwood of both American basswood *(Tilia americana)* and white basswood *(T. heterophylla)*. The heartwood is pale yellowish brown with occasional darker streaks. Sapwood is wide and creamy-white or pale brown that merges gradually into the heartwood. Soft and light in weight. Fine, even texture. Straight-grained and easy to work with tools. Shrinkage in width and thickness during drying is rated as large; however, basswood seldom warps in use. Used mainly in venetian blinds, sash and door frames, molding and veneer.

Beech *(Fagus)* Beech varies in color from nearly white sapwood to reddish-brown heartwood in some trees. Sometimes there is no clear demarcation between heartwood and sapwood, which may be three to five inches thick. The wood has little figure and is of close, uniform texture. Heavy, strong, hard, high in resistance to shock, and highly suitable for steam bending. Shrinks substantially and therefore requires careful drying. Machines smoothly, excellent for turning, wears well, and easily treated with preservatives. Largely used for flooring, furniture, handles and veneer.

Birch The important species of birch are yellow birch *(Betula alleghaniensis)*, sweet birch *(B. lenta)* and paper birch *(B. papyrifera)*. Other birches of some commercial importance are river birch *(B. nigra)*, gray birch *(B. populifolia)* and western paper birch *(B. papyrifera var. communtata)*. Yellow birch has white sapwood (sometimes called "white birch") and light reddish-brown heartwood. Sweet birch has light-colored sapwood and dark brown heartwood tinged with red. Wood of yellow birch and sweet birch is heavy, hard, strong and has good shock resistance. Fine and uniform in texture. Paper birch is lower in weight, softer and lower in strength than yellow and sweet birch. Birch shrinks considerably during drying. Yellow and sweet birch lumber are often used for furniture, interior finish and doors. Birch veneer goes into plywood used for flush doors, furniture and paneling.

Brazilian Cherry (see Cherry)

Butternut *(Juglans cinerea)* Also called white walnut, butternut has a narrow, nearly white sapwood and heartwood which is light brown, frequently modified by pinkish tones or darker brown streaks. Moderately light in weight, rather coarse-textured, moderately weak in bending and endwise compression, relatively low in stiffness. Machines easily and finishes well. In many ways resembles black walnut when stained, but does not have the strength or hardness. A principal use is veneer which is further manufactured into furniture, cabinets and paneling.

California Redwood (see Redwood)

Carpathian Elm, or American Elm (see Elm)

Cedar *(Cedrus)* (see Alaska-Cedar)

Cherry Primarily known as black cherry *(Prunus serotina)*, or sometimes as wild black cherry or wild cherry. Heartwood varies from light to dark reddish brown and has a distinctive luster. Sapwood is narrow in old trees and nearly white. Fairly uniform texture with good machining properties. Moderately heavy, strong, stiff, moderately hard, high shock resistance and moderately large shrinkage. After seasoning, very dimensionally stable. Used principally for furniture, fine veneer panels and architectural woodwork.

Dade County Pine (see Pine, Southern)

Douglas-Fir *(Pseudotsuga menziesii)* Also known as red-fir, Douglas-spruce and yellow-fir. Sapwood is narrow in old-growth trees but may be as much as three inches wide in second-growth trees of commercial size. Fairly young trees of moderate to rapid growth have reddish heartwood and are called red-fir. Very narrow-ringed wood of old trees may be yellowish brown and is known on the market as yellow-fir. Wood varies widely in weight and strength. When lumber of high strength is needed for structural uses, selection can be improved by applying the density rule. This rule uses percentage of latewood and rate of growth as they affect density. The higher density generally indicates stronger wood. Used mostly for building and construction in the form of lumber, timber, piles and plywood. Also used in the manufacture of sash, doors, laminated beams, general millwork, flooring and furniture. Douglas-fir plywood has found ever-increasing usefulness in the construction of furniture and cabinets.

Eastern White Maple (see Maple, Silver)

Eastern White Pine (see Pine)

Ebony *(Diospyros)* Mostly known as a dark black wood, Macassar ebony is medium-brown to dark-brown with black stripes, and coromandel ebony is brown with gray or brown mottling. Texture is fine and even. Extremely heavy. Hard and brittle, but can be machine finished to a high luster. Especially useful for furniture and carving.

Elm *(Ulmus)* Occurring widely in the northern hemisphere, the various species of elm are generally similar. The sapwood is nearly white and the heartwood light brown, often tinged with red. Divided into two general classes, hard elm and soft elm, depending on the weight and strength of the wood. Hard elm includes rock elm, winged elm, cedar elm and September elm. American elm and slippery elm are the soft elms. Soft elm is moderately heavy, has high shock resistance and is moderately hard and stiff. Hard elm species are somewhat heavier than soft elm. All species have excellent bending qualities. Elm lumber and elm veneer are often used for furniture.

English Pine (see Pine)

Eucalyptus Saligna (see Saligna Gum)

European Cherry (see Cherry)

European Walnut (see Walnut)

European White Birch (see Birch)

French Walnut (see Walnut)

Greenheart *(Ocotea rodiaei)* Pale yellow-green to dark olive-brown, frequently with dark, almost black, markings. Fine, even texture. Straight, interlocked grain. Dense, exceptionally strong, with almost twice the strength of oak for bending, compression and stiffness. Difficult to machine. Resistant to decay. Often used for decking.

Hard Maple (see Maple)

Honduras Mahogany (see Mahogany)

Incienso A South American name used for many woods, such as Myrocarpus and Myroxylon. "Balsamo" is another common name for this group of scented woods.

Japanese Maple (see Maple)

Koa *(Acacia koa)* Native to Hawaii, this large tree grows to one hundred feet in height. The heartwood of mature trees varies from rich red to golden brown and may have a satiny luster. The sapwood is yellowish-white. Uses include furniture, cabinetry and calabashes.

Lacewood *(Cardwellia sublimis)* Also known as silky oak, selano, Australian silky oak, northern silky oak. Heartwood is pale pink to pinkish brown, with a distinct silvery sheen. The color upon exposure turns brown. Moderately hard and heavy. Coarse texture. Straight grain. The most prominent feature of a lacewood surface is that it has large rays, which result in a small, flaky grain pattern considered attractive for decorative purposes. Light and soft, yet firm, strong and tough. Good for steam bending. Moderately durable. Works easily by hand and machine tools. Stains readily and finishes fairly well. The large rays tend to give trouble with crumbling. Used as a highly ornamental wood for cabinetry and flooring.

Lodgepole Pine (see Pine)

Macassar Ebony (see Ebony)

Mahogany The name mahogany is presently applied to several distinct kinds of commercial woods. The original mahogany wood, produced by the genus Swietenia, came from the West Indies; in Europe during the 1600s it was the premier wood for fine furniture, cabinet work and ship-building. Because the good reputation associated with the name mahogany is based on this wood, American mahogany, or Honduras mahogany, is sometimes referred to as true mahogany. A related African wood, of the genus Khaya, has long been marketed as "African mahogany" and the similar properties and overall appearance allow it to be used for much of the same purposes as American mahogany. A third kind of mahogany, and the one most commonly encountered in the market, is "Philippine mahogany." This name is applied to a group of Asian woods belonging to three distinct genera: Shorea, Parashorea and Pentacme. Projects in this work have featured only that mahogany which is known as American mahogany, or Honduras mahogany, or true mahogany (*Swietenia macrophylla*). The heartwood varies from a pale pink or salmon color to a dark reddish brown. Grain is usually straighter than that of African mahogany; however, a wide variety of grain patterns is obtained from mahogany. Texture is rather fine to coarse. Easily air-seasoned or kiln-dried without appreciable warping or checking. Excellent dimensional stability properties. Durable in resistance to decay fungi and moderately resistant to dry-wood termites. Both heartwood and sapwood are resistant to impregnation with preservatives. Easy to work by hand or machine tools. Slices into fine veneer without difficulty. Easy to finish and takes an excellent polish. Used for fine furniture and cabinetmaking, interior trim, fancy veneers, paneling and carving.

Maple Commercial species include sugar maple (*Acer saccharum*), black maple (*A. nigrum*), silver maple (*A. saccharinum*), red maple (*A. rubrum*), boxelder (*A. negundo*) and bigleaf maple (*A. macrophyllum*). Japanese maple is mainly *A. mono*. Sugar maple is also known as hard maple and rock maple; black maple as black sugar maple; silver maple as white maple, river maple, water maple and swamp maple; red maple as soft maple, water maple, scarlet maple, white maple and swamp maple; boxelder as ash-leaved maple, three-leaved maple and cut-leaved maple; and bigleaf maple as Oregon maple. The wood of sugar maple and black maple is known as hard maple; that of silver maple, red maple and boxelder as soft maple. Sapwood is commonly white with a slight reddish-brown tinge, and three to five or more inches thick. Heartwood is usually light reddish brown, but sometimes is considerably darker. Hard maple has a fine, uniform texture and is heavy, strong, stiff, hard, resistant to shock, and has large shrinkage. Sugar maple is usually straight-grained, but the grain also occurs as "bird's-eye," "curly" and "fiddleback" grain. Soft maple is not as heavy as hard maple, but has been substituted for hard maple in the better grades, particularly for furniture. In addition to furniture, maple is often used for flooring.

Oak *(Red Oak Group)* Principal species are: northern red oak (*Quercus rubra*), scarlet oak (*Q. coccinea*), shumard oak (*Q. shumardii*), pin oak (*Q. palustris*), nuttall oak (*Q. nuttallii*), black oak (*Q. velutina*), southern red oak (Q. falcata), cherrybark oak (*Q. falcata var. pagodaefolia*), water oak (*Q. nigra*), laurel oak (*Q. laurifolia*), and willow oak (*Q. phellos*). Sapwood is nearly white and usually one to two inches thick. Heartwood is brown with a tinge of red. Sawed lumber of red oak cannot be separated by species on the basis of the characteristics of the wood alone. Red oak lumber can be separated from white oak by the size and arrangement of pores in latewood and because, as a rule, it lacks tyloses in the pores. Quartersawn lumber of oaks is distinguished by broad and conspicuous rays, which add to its attractiveness. Wood of red oaks is heavy. Rapidly grown second-growth oak is generally harder and tougher than finer-textured old-growth timber. Red oaks have fairly large shrinkage in drying. Often used for flooring, furniture and general millwork.

Oak *(White Oak Group)* Principal species are: white oak (*Quercus alba*), chestnut oak (*Q. prinus*), post oak (*Q. stellata*), overcup oak (*Q. lyrata*), swamp chestnut oak (*Q. michauxii*), bur oak (*Q. macrocarpa*), chinkapin oak (*Q. muehlenbergii*), swamp white oak (*Q. bicolor*), and live oak (*Q. virginiana*). Heartwood of white oaks is generally grayish brown, and the sapwood, which is one to two or more inches thick, is nearly white. The pores of the heartwood of white oaks are usually plugged with tyloses, tending to make the wood impenetrable by liquids. The exception is chestnut oak, which lacks tyloses in many of its pores. The wood of white oak is heavy, averaging somewhat higher in weight than that of the red oaks. The heartwood has moderately good decay resistance. Live oak is considerably heavier and stronger than the other oaks. Often used in flooring, furniture, doors and millwork.

Oriented Fir Strandboard (see Strandboard)

Padauk *(Pterocarpus)* Brightly colored, with the African padauk being purple-red when first sawn, then darkening to a deep purple-brown. Typically coarse in texture, with an interlocked grain. Heavy or moderately heavy. High resistance to decay. East Indian padauk, highly figured, is known as "amboyna."

Parota *(Enterolobium cyclocarpum)* Similar to saman, and sometimes called "monkey pod" or "raintree," parota is a tree with brown heartwood of various shadings, sometimes with a reddish tinge, which is sharply demarcated from the whitish sapwood. The grain typically is interlocked and the texture is coarse. Native to the Mexican states of Michoacan, Jalisco and Guerrero.

Pau Marfim *(Balfourodendron riedelianum)* With a rather limited growing range, extending from Brazil into Paraguay and northern Argentina, pau marfim is known by that name in Argentina, but as guatambu in Paraguay. The wood's color and general appearance is similar to birch or hard maple sapwood, but with less distinct growth rings. Easy to work and finish, but not resistant to decay. No apparent difference in color between heartwood and sapwood.

Pear *(Pyrus communis)* A northern temperate tree widely cultivated for its fruit, pearwood is a pale pink-brown. Its texture is unifirm and fine, with a grain straight or irregular, depending on the stem's shape. Moderately heavy, similar to beech.

Pine Eastern white pine (*Pinus strobus*) is also known as white pine, northern white pine, Weymouth pine and soft pine. Heartwood is light brown, often with a reddish tinge. Turns considerably darker on exposure. Wood has comparatively uniform texture and is straight-grained. Easily kiln- dried, has small shrinkage and ranks high in stability. Easy to work and can be readily glued. Light in weight, moderately soft, moderately low in strength and low in resistance to shock. Uses include sash, doors, furniture, trim, finish and knotty paneling. Lodgepole pine (*P. contoria*), is also known as knotty pine, black pine, spruce pine and jack pine. Heartwood varies from light yellow to light yellow-brown. Sapwood is yellow or nearly white. Wood is generally straight-grained, with narrow growth rings. Moderately light in weight, fairly easy to work, and has moderately large shrinkage. Moderately low in strength, moderately soft, moderately stiff and moderately low in shock resistance. Used for framing, siding, finish and flooring. Radiata pine (*P. radiata*), a plantation species from the south temperate region, has a pinkish-brown heartwood, although its sapwood is pale. Growth rings are mostly wide and distinct. False rings may be common. Texture is moderately even and fine. Grain is usually straight. Varies in weight but usually compares closely with European redwood. Dries quickly. Stable in use. Strong for its weight and works well, though tending to tear near its knots. Not durable. The better-quality wood is used for furniture, plywood, fiberboard, particleboard and millwork. Southern pine includes a number of species: longleaf pine (*P. palustris*), shortleaf pine (*P. echinata*), loblolly pine (*P. taeda*), and slash pine (*P. elliotti*). Lumber from any one or a mixture of these is classified as southern pine in the industry. Lumber that is produced from longleaf and slash pine species are classified as longleaf within the U.S. and as pitch pine in the export trade. The wood of all these southern pines is similar: yellowish white sapwood and reddish brown heartwood. Sapwood is usually wide in second-growth stands. Longleaf and slash pine are classified as heavy, strong, stiff, hard and moderately high in shock resistance. Shortleaf and loblolly pine are usually somewhat lighter in weight than longleaf. All the southern pines have moderately large shrinkage but are stable when properly seasoned. Among uses of the lower density southern pines are interior finish and structural grade plywood.

Poplar *(Populus)* (see Yellow-Poplar)

Purpleheart (see Amaranth)

Radiata Pine (see Pine)

Red Alder *(Alnus rubra)* The wood of red alder varies from almost white to pale pinkish brown and has no visible boundary between heartwood and sapwood. It is moderately light in weight, intermediate in most strength properties, but low in shock resistance. Relatively low shrinkage. Used principally for furniture, but also used for sash, doors, panel stock and millwork.

Red Cedar Eastern red cedar (*Juniperus virginiana*) and another species, southern red cedar (*J. silicicola*), have heartwood that is bright red or dull red, and the thin sapwood is nearly white. Wood is moderately heavy, moderately low in strength, hard, and high in shock resistance, but low in stiffness. Very small shrinkage and stays in place after seasoning. Fine and uniform texture. Usually straight grain, except where deflected by knots, which are numerous. Eastern red cedar heartwood is very resistant to decay. Used for fenceposts, and lumber is manufactured into chests, wardrobes, closet lining and flooring. Western red cedar (*Thuja plicata*), also called canoe-cedar, giant arborvitae, shinglewood and Pacific red cedar, has heartwood that is reddish or pinkish brown to dull brown and sapwood that is nearly white. The sapwood is narrow, often not more than one inch in width. The wood is generally straight-grained and has a uniform but rather coarse texture. Very small shrinkage. Light in weight, moderately soft, low in strength when used as beams or posts. Low in shock resistance. Its heartwood is very resistant to decay. Used principally for shingles, lumber, poles, posts and piles. The lumber is used for exterior siding, interior finish, greenhouse construction, sash, doors and millwork.

Red Oak (see Oak)

Redwood *(Sequoia sempervirens)* A very large tree, closely related to the giant sequoia *(Sequoiadendron giganteum)*. Other names for redwood are coast redwood, California redwood and sequoia. Heartwood varies from a light cherry to a dark mahogany. The narrow sapwood is almost white. Typical old-growth redwood is moderately light in weight, moderately strong and stiff, and moderately hard. The wood is easy to work, generally straight-grained, and shrinks and swells comparatively little. Heartwood from old-growth trees has high decay resistance, but heartwood from second-growth trees generally ranges from resistant to moderately decay resistant. Most redwood lumber is used for building. It is remanufactured extensively into siding, sash, doors, blinds, finish and outdoor furniture. Some redwood veneer is manufactured for decorative plywood.

Rock Maple (see Maple)

Saligna Gum *(Eucalyptus saligna)* Native to Australia, where it is known as blue gum and now planted in many parts of the world, Saligna wood is heavy, and its color is medium-red to dark-red. Young trees are lighter in weight and have a pale pink wood. Typically straight-grained, with a fairly fine and even texture. Dries fairly quickly and then can be machined to a good finish. Its strength, durability and working properties vary considerably, with the lighter wood being perishable. Used often for flooring and fiberboard.

Sapele *(Entandrophragma cylindricum)* A large African rainforest tree, its heartwood ranges in color from that of mahogany to a dark reddish or purplish brown. The lighter colored and distinct sapwood may be up to four inches thick. Texture is rather fine. Grain in interlocked and produces a narrow and uniform stripe pattern on quartered surfaces. Works fairly easily with machine tools, although interlocked grain offers difficulties in planing and molding. Finishes and glues well. The heartwood is rated as moderately durable and resistant to preservative treatment. Used primarily as veneer for decorative plywood, but also in the solid form for furniture and cabinetwork, joinery and flooring.

Silver Maple (see Maple)

Sitka Spruce *(Picea sitchensis)* Also known as yellow spruce, tideland spruce, western spruce, silver spruce and west coast spruce. Heartwood is a light pinkish brown. The sapwood, which may be three to six incches wide or even wider in young trees, is creamy white and shades gradually into the heartwood. The wood has a comparatively fine, uniform texture and generally straight grain. Moderately light in weight, moderately low in bending and compressive strength, moderately stiff, moderately soft, and moderately low in resistance to shock. Moderately small shrinkage. On the basis of weight, it rates high in strength properties and can be obtained in clear, straight-grained pieces. Important uses include furniture, sash, doors, blinds and millwork.

Standboard (also Particleboard, Chipboard, Flakeboard, and Fiberboard) Composite products made of wood parts arranged in various ways. When they are defined as being "oriented," their individual particles are oriented in a particular way to provide additional strength.

Sugar Maple (see Maple)

Sycamore (see Plane)

Tasmanian Oak (see Oak)

Teak *(Tectona grandis)* Heartwood varies from yellow brown to dark golden brown and eventually turns a rich brown color upon exposure. Coarse uneven textures (ring porous), usually straight-grained, with a distinctly oily feel. Heartwood has excellent dimensional stability and possesses a very high degree of natural durability. Generally worked with moderate ease with hand and machine tools. However, silica in the wood often dulls tools. Finishing and gluing are satisfactory, although pretreatment may be necessary to ensure good bonding of finishes and glues. Unique in that it does not cause rust or erosion when in contact with metal. Uses include furniture, flooring, decorative objects and veneer from decorative plywood.

Walnut *(Juglans)* European walnut *(J. regia)* is gray-brown with almost black streaks and generally more variable in color than American walnut *(J. nigra)*, which is usually dark, purple-brown. Straight or occasionally wavy grain. Medium texture. Slightly lighter than beech in weight. Moderately stable. Works easily and is noted for its excellent finish. Moderately resistant to fungi. Used for cabinetwork, furniture and decorative paneling, primarily as veneer.

Western Red Cedar (see Red Cedar)

White Alder (see Alder, Red)

White Ash (see Ash)

White Birch (see Birch)

White Oak (see Oak)

White Pine (see Eastern White Pine)

Yellow Birch (see Birch)

Yellow Cedar (see Alaska-Cedar)

Yellow Pine (see Eastern White Pine)

Yellow-Poplar *(Liriodendron tulipifera)* Also known as poplar, tulip-poplar and tulipwood. Sapwood, sometimes called white poplar or whitewood, is white and frequently several inches thick. Heartwood is yellowish brown, sometimes streaked with purple, green, black, blue or red. These colorations do not affect the wood's physical properties. Generally straight-grained and comparatively uniform in texture. Old-growth timber is moderately light in weight and moderately low in bending strength, moderately soft and moderately low in shock resistance. Moderately large shrinkage when dried from a green condition but not difficult to season and stays in place well after seasoning. Much of the second-growth yellow-poplar is heavier, harder and stronger than old-growth. Lumber often used for furniture, interior finish and siding. Also made into plywood which is used for paneling, furniture and other specialty products. Lumber from the cucumbertree *(Magnolia acuminata)* is sometimes included in shipments of yellow-poplar because of its similarity.

Wood Words

Reprinted, with some deletions, from:
Architectural Woodwork Quality Standards, 6th Edition, Version 1.1
Published by
The Architectural Woodwork Institute
Department G
P.O. Box 1550
Centreville, Virginia 22020

Acrylic Lacquers In finishing, high-quality clear system for finishing furniture.

Adhesives 1. Type I adhesives are exterior glues and must withstand a bond test described in ANSI/NWWDA 1S-1 Series. (ANSI is the American National Standards Institute. NWWDA is the National Wood Window and Door Association.)
2. Type II adhesives are interior glues and must withstand a bond test described in ANSI/NWWDA 1S-1 Series.

Adjustable Shelves Generally accomplished through the use of multiple holes with either plastic or metal pins to hold the shelves.

Architectural Woodwork Fine custom woodworking, so varied in design and complexity that it becomes difficult to define, specified for special applications and functions by design professionals and created by woodworkers. It includes all exterior and interior woodwork exposed to view in a finished building (except lumberyard or specialty items of flooring, shingles, exposed roof decking, ceiling, siding, structural wood trusses and rafters, and overhead-type doors), including all exposed wood, plywood, high- and low-pressure decorative laminates and wood doors.
    Items made of other materials are included only if called for in the specifications. Finishing may be included if specified. Site installation may also be included if specified.

Articulated Joint In architectural paneling, joint details that allow for field variations.

Back Veneer The veneer placed on the semi-exposed or concealed face of a veneered panel construction to balance the construction. Also, the side reverse to the face of a panel, or the poorer side of panel in any grade calling for a face and a back.

Balance Match Two or more veneer components or leaves of equal size (prior to edge trimming) to make up a single face. Generally most aesthetically pleasing.

Balanced Construction To achieve balanced construction, panels should be absolutely symmetrical from the center line; i.e., use materials on either side which contract or expand, or are moisture-permeable, at the same rate.
    Balancing sheet requirements for high-pressure decorative laminate fabrication vary with the product. Doors and free-hanging or free-standing panels should have the same laminate on the back as on the face, and applied in the same machine direction. Tops or cabinet members, on the other hand, merely require some form of balancing material.

Baluster In stairwork, the vertical members that support the handrail.

Barber Pole An effect in book-matching of veneers resulting from tight and loose sides of veneers having different light reflections when finished.

Bark Pocket Comparatively small area of bark around which normal wood has grown.

Base Moldings Generally a molding placed around a door frame or window frame. Moldings used to trim the intersection of a wall or cabinet and the floor.

Base Shoes A small molding combined with a base molding to complete the trimming of the wall and floor intersection.

Bleaching In finishing, the removal of color or whitening of the substrate.

Blending Color change that is detectable at a distance of six to eight feet but which does not seriously detract from the overall appearance of the panel.

Block Free In finishing, means material has dried sufficiently so that finished items do not stick together.

Blocking Commonly understood as the wooden support material placed within or upon gypsum board and plaster walls to support cabinetry.

Board Foot A piece of wood one inch thick, twelve inches long and twelve inches wide, or its equivalent (144 cubic inches). When stock is less than one inch thick it is usually calculated as if it were a full one inch thick.

Book Match Matching between adjacent veneer leaves on one panel face. Every other piece of veneer is turned over, so that adjacent leaves are "opened" as two pages in a book.

Burl A swirl or twist in the grain of the wood which usually occurs near a knot or crotch but does not contain a knot.

Butcher Block Generally refers to face laminate hardwoods (usually maple) forming a work surface in which the edge grain is exposed to wear.

Casework Base and wall cabinets, display fixtures and storage shelves. The generic term for both "boxes" and special desks, reception counters, nurses stations and the like. Generally includes the tops and work surfaces.

Casings Generally a molding placed around a door frame or window frame.

Catalyzed In finishing, an ingredient added to a basic product to provide additional performance characteristics.

Center Match Each panel has an even number of veneer leaves of uniform width. Thus, there is a veneer joint in the center of each panel, producing horizontal symmetry. A small amount of the figure is lost. This method increases waste and, consequently, cost.

Chair Rails A decorative molding placed at a height on the wall comparable to the place where the back of a chair would impact the wall surface.

Checks Small slits running parallel to grain of wood, caused chiefly by strains produced in seasoning.

Chip Core See particleboard core.

Cleats In closet and utility shelving, the wood members furnished to support the shelf.

Comb Grain A quality rift veneer with exceptionally straight grain and closely spaced growth increments.

Component *(of face)* An individual piece of veneer that is jointed to other pieces to achieve a full length and width face. Terms used interchangeably with component in the context of face are piece and leaf.

Concealed Surfaces In casework, surfaces are considered concealed when:
    surfaces are not visible after installation; bottoms of cabinets less than thirty inches above
    finished floor; tops of cabinets over 78 inches above finished floor and not visible from an
    upper level; stretchers, blocking and components concealed by drawers.

Contact Cement Normally used for bonding high-pressure decorative laminates to a substrate.

Conversion Varnish In finishing, a class of coatings that are tough and exhibit excellent resistance to household chemicals.

Core Flush doors and plywood are said to have a "core" material and/or construction. Typical cores are lumber core (also known as stave lumber core); veneer core; particleboard core; or fiberboard core.

Cope To cut or shape the end of a molded wood member so that it will cover and fit the contour of the sticking coping at the joint.

Cove Moldings Similar to crown moldings, often smaller in size and less decorative.

Crossbar Type of figure or irregularity of grain resembling a dip in grain running at right angles, or nearly so, to the length of the veneer component.

Crown Moldings Moldings used to accent ceiling intersections and traditional pediments and casework tops.

Custom Grade The middle or normal grade in both material and workmanship, and intended for high-quality, conventional work.

Dado Joint A groove cut across the grain of the face of a member to receive the edge or end thickness of another member.

Decay The decomposition of wood substance by fungi.

Delamination Separation of plies or layers of wood or other materials through failure of the adhesive joint.

Distressing In finishing, either a mechanical or chemical special effect.

Dovetail Joints 1. Multi-finger -- used to form a corner joint (e.g. drawer construction).
2. Through Dovetail or French Dovetail -- similar to a dado, a form of locking joint.

Dowel Joint When short, round wooden pegs or pins are inserted into predrilled holes to reinforce edge or butt joints. Strength is similar to that of mortise and tenon joints.

Doze *(synonymous with Dote)* A form of incipient decay characterized by a dull and lifeless appearance of wood, accompanied by a lack of strength and softening of the wood substance.

Drawings 1. Part of the project documents put in place by the owner and/or design professionals which, in combination with written specifications, define the scope, quality assurance, requirements, submittals, field dimensions, product handling and product specifications to the woodworker.
2. Shop drawings are detailed engineering drawings produced by the woodworker for the fabrication of the architectural woodwork products, and often submitted to the owner and/or design professional for approval.

Easement In stairwork, a short bend changing direction or pitch of a handrail.

Economy Grade The lower grade in both material and workmanship, and intended to work where price outweighs quality considerations.

Edge Joint When the edges of boards are glued together to increase the width.

End Butt Joint 1. When one end is glued to an edge or face of another board to form an angle (e.g., stiles and rails of a face frame).
2. When the end of one board is fastened to the end of another to increase its length (e.g., running trim).

End Match Matching between adjacent veneer leaves on one panel face. Veneer leaves are book-matched end to end as well as side to side. Generally used for very tall panels or for projects in which only short-length veneers are available.

Exposed Surfaces In casework, surfaces visible when:
    drawers and opaque doors (if any) are closed; behind clear glass doors; bottoms of cabinets
    42 inches or more above finished floor; tops of cabinets below 78 inches above finished floor.

Face The better side of any panel in which the outer plies are of different veneer grades. Also either side of a panel in which there is no difference in veneer grades.

Face Joint When the faces of boards are glued together to increase the thickness.

Fiberboard Core Manufactured from wood reduced to fine fibers mixed with binders and formed by the use of heat and pressure into panels.

Figure The pattern produced, usually across the grain, by natural deviations from the normal grain.

Filler In finishing, is used to close the pores of wood.

Finger Joint   When the ends of two pieces of lumber are cut to an identically matching set. Used most commonly to increase the length of the board.

Fire Rated   Fire-retardant particleboard is available with an Underwriters Laboratory (UL) stamp for Class 1 fire rating (Flame Spread 20, Smoke Developed 25). Fire-rated doors are available with particleboard and mineral cores for ratings up to one-and-a-half hours. It is the responsibility of the specifier to indicate what fire retardant classification is required for a particular product. In the absence of such a specified rating, the woodworker may supply unrated product.

Fire Retardant Treatment   Only a few species are treated with chemicals to reduce flammability and retard the spread of flame over the surface. This usually involves impregnation of the wood, under pressure, with salts and other chemicals. White oak is untreatable.

Flakeboard   See particleboard.

Flake, Ray   Portion of a medullary ray as it appears on the quarter-cut surface. Flake can be a dominant feature in oak and is sometimes referred to as fleck.

Flamespread Classification   The generally accepted measurement for fire rating of materials. It compares the rate of flamespread on a particular species with the rate of flamespread on untreated red oak.

Flat Slicing   See plain slicing.

Flitch   The veneer slices of one half log, kept in order, used for the production of fine plywood panels. To determine the approximate amount of face veneer required, multiply the panel surface area by three. This ratio may have to be increased to accommodate exacting requirements of appearance when the flitch contains a wide range of characteristics.

Flush Construction   Cabinet construction in which door and drawer faces are set within and flush with the body members of face frames of the cabinet with spaces between face surfaces sufficient for operating clearance.

Flush Overlay   Cabinet construction in which door and drawer faces cover the body members of the cabinet with spaces between face surfaces sufficient for operating clearance.

Glazing   In finishing, an added step for achieving color or heightening grain appearance.

Grading Rules   Most hardwoods are graded utilizing the rules established by the National Hardwood Lumber Association. Softwoods, on the other hand, are graded by several grading associations. The three primary softwood grading associations in the United States are Western Wood Products Association, Southern Pine Inspection Bureau and Redwood Inspection Service.

Although lumber must be purchased by the woodworker according to these grading rules, these rules should not be used to specify lumber for architectural woodwork.

Softwood Plywood is graded by the American Plywood Association. Grade markings are stamped on the back or edge of each sheet. Hardwood Plywood is made under the standards of the Hardwood Plywood and Veneer Association. These grades are rarely marked on the panels.

Grain   Arrangement of wood fibers and pores evident on cut and/or finished wood products. The direction, size, arrangement and apearance of the fibers in wood or veneer. The appearance of the grain varies with both the species and the cut.

Grain Slope   Expression of the angle of the grain to the long edges of the veneer component.

Grain Sweep   Expression of the angle of the grain to the long edges of the veneer component over the area extending one-eighth of the length of the piece from the ends.

Gum Pockets   Well-defined openings between rings of annual growth, containing gum or evidence of prior gum accumulations.

Gum Spots   Gum or color spots caused by prior resin accumulations sometimes found on panel surfaces.

Hairline   Thin, perceptible line showing at the joint of two pieces of wood.

Half Round   A method of cutting veneers on an off-center lathe that results in modified characteristics of both rotary and plain sliced veneers. Often used in red and white oak.

Hand-Rubbed Finish   In finishing, a manual step performed to smooth, flatten or dull the topcoat.

Handrail   In stairwork, the member which follows the pitch of the stair for grasping by the hand.

Hardboard   Constructed of inter-felted fibers consolidated and formed under heat and pressure into panels.

Hardware   Cabinet hardware is generally furnished and installed by the woodworker. Window hardware must be specified, as it dictates the details of construction.

Hardwood   Generally obtained from deciduous trees. Does not refer to the specific density or resistance to wear and abuse.

Heartwood   The inactive cells of the inner tree, located below the sapwood. The cell cavities of the heartwood may contain deposits which make it darker in color than the sapwood.

High-Pressure Decorative Laminate   Melamine and phenolic resin-impregnated papers with decorative surfaces protected by a clear melamine coating.

Inconspicuous   Barely detectable with the naked eye at a distance of six to eight feet.

Intumescent Coatings   Can be applied to the surface of flammable products to reduce flammability. Generally difficult to use and rather fragile. Highly hygroscopic.

KCPI   Abbreviation for knife cuts per inch. Generally used when describing the result of molded profiles or materials which are surfaced on four sides.

Knot   Cross section of tree branch or limb with grain usually running at right angles to that of the piece of wood in which it occurs.

Knots, Blending Pin   Sound knots one-fourth inch or less in diameter that do not contain dark centers.

Blending pin knots are detectable at a distance of six to eight feet and do not seriously detract from the overall appearance of the panel.

Knots, Pin   Sound knots one-fourth inch or less in diameter containing dark centers.

Knots, Sound, Tight   Knots that are solid across their face and fixed by growth to retain their place.

Lemon Spline   Used to join wood members.

Lights (*Lites*)   In door construction, beaded openings to receive glazing.

Locking Joint   There are many variations of this joint. The joint is produced when the adjoining pieces are machined into a locking form.

Louvers   In door construction, openings fitted with metal or wood louver panels.

LPDL   Abbreviation for low pressure decorative laminate.

Lumber   Produced from a living, growing material; and graded for sale by grading rules.

Matching Within Panel Face   The individual leaves of veneer in a sliced flitch increase or decrease in width as the slicing progresses. Thus, if a number of panels are manufactured from a particular flitch, the number of veneer leaves per panel face will change as the flitch is utilized.

Medium-Density Overlay   A panel product particularly well suited for opaque (paint) finishes.

Medium-Density Particleboard   Generally refers to particleboard manufactured to an approximate density of 45 pounds per cubic foot. The type of particleboard used for architectural woodworking substrates.

Mirror Polish Finish   In finishing, several steps of wet sanding, mechanical buffing and polishing.

Miter Joint   When two surfaces are cut at any angle (typically 45 degrees).

Modular Casework   Casework produced from a manufacturer's standard details adapted to use for a particular project.

Moisture Content   The amount of water contained in wood, expressed as a percentage that indicates the relative weight of the water in the piece compared to the oven dry weight. The optimum moisture content of wood for interior use is between 5 and 13 percent depending on the part of the country.

Mortise and Tenon Joint   When one piece is slotted (mortise) to fit the tongue (tenon) of the adjoining piece.

Newel Post   In stairwork, an upright post that supports or receives the handrail at critical points of the stair, such as starting, landing or top.

NGR Stains   Refers to non-grain-raising stains.

Nominal Measurements   The average sizes (width and thickness) of lumber just out of the sawmill, before being processed into usable board stock. Always larger than "finished" dimensions.

Nosing   In stairwork, the shaped edge, or edges, of tread or landing.

Orange Peel   In finishing, slight depressions in surface, similar to the skin of an orange.

Panel Products   Manufactured panels used in architectural woodwork, not to be confused with panels formed by the edge gluing of solid lumber with any facings adhered thereto.

Panelwork   Includes stile and rail paneling and all kinds of flush panel work made of lumber panel products and high-pressure decorative laminates.

Particleboard Core   This term also includes flakeboard and chipboard. Manufactured from natural wood reduced particles, fibers and chips mixed with binders and formed by the use of heat and pressure into panels.

Penetrating Oil   In finishing, an oil-based material designed to penetrate the wood.

Permalam®   The registered collective trademark of members of American Laminators Association used to indicate decorative laminates conforming to The Performance Standard for Thermoset Decorative Panels, ALA 1992.

Phenol Formaldehyde Resin   Typically used for exterior type construction. Plywood and doors bonded with this adhesive have a high resistance to moisture. The most common types require high temperatures during pressing to aid in the curing process.

Plain Sawn   Yields broad grain pattern, widest boards and least waste from the log.

Plain Slicing   Most common for hardwood plywood, the log is cut in half. One half is placed onto a carriage and moved up and down past a fixed knife to produce the veneers. Veneer sliced parallel to the plith of the log and approximately tangent to the growth rings to achieve flat cut veneer. Each piece is generally placed in a stack and kept in order. One half log, sliced this way, is called a flitch.

Plastic Laminate Finish   See high-pressure laminate finish, and high-pressure decorative laminate.

Pleasing Matched   A face containing components which provides a pleasing overall appearance. The grain of the various components need not be matched at the joints. Sharp color contrasts at the joints of the components are not permitted.

Plough Joint   A groove cut with the grain of the face of a member to receive the edge or end thickness of another member.

Polyester   In finishing, a very high solids content plastic coating, leaving a deep wet look.

Polyurethane   In finishing, usually a two-component system that has a higher solids content than lacquers.

Premium Grade   The highest grade available in both material and workmanship intended for the finest work. This is naturally the most expensive grade.

Preservatives   All lumber species used for exterior architectural woodwork, except the heartwood of Redwood and Western Red Cedar (although it is desirable for those species) shall be treated to provide long-term protection.

PVC   Abbreviation for polyvinyl chloride, a synthetic decorative coating or edge banding.

Quality Certification   The Architectural Woodwork Institute (AWI) in cooperation with the American Arbitration Association (AAA) will maintain an inspection service which will be available to specifiers of our industry products produced or manufactured within the continental boundaries of the United States. This program is available on any project where specifications reference Architectural Woodwork Institute Quality Standards.

Quality Standards   For architectural woodwork, this term generally refers to the Architectural Woodwork Institute (AWI) Quality Standards, Guide Specifications and Quality Certification Program, published and revised regularly by AWI.

Quarter Sawn   Refers to solid lumber cutting. Available in limited amounts in certain species. Yields straight grain, narrow boards, "flake" or figure in some species. More expensive than plain sawn.

Quarter Slicing   Produces a striped grain pattern, straight in some woods, varied in others. Veneer produced by cutting in a radial direction to the pith to the extent that ray flake is produced, and the amount may be unlimited. In some woods, principally oak, "flake" results from cutting through the radial "rays."

Quarters   The commercial thicknesses usually associated with the purchase or specification of hardwoods, such as "five quarter" (5/4 of one inch), meaning one and one quarter inches in thickness.

Rabbet Joint   A groove cut across the grain of the face of a member at an edge or end to receive the edge or end thickness of another member.

Railings   In stairwork, the member that follows the pitch of the stair for grasping by the hand.

Raised Panel   Traditional door or wall panel with a bevel edge captured in a stile and rail frame.

Random Match   Matching between adjacent veneer leaves on one panel face. Random selection in the arrangement of veneer leaves from one or more flitches producing a deliberate mismatch between the pieces of veneer.

Red Birch   The heartwood of the Yellow Birch tree.

Repairs   A patch, shim or filler material inserted and/or glued into veneer or a panel to achieve a sound surface.

Repairs, Blending   Wood or filler insertions similar in color to adjacent wood so as to blend well.

Resorcinol Formaldehyde Resin   For woodworking, formulated into highly water-resistant glues, usually purple in color and difficult to work.

Return   Continuation in a different direction of a molding or projection, usually right angles.

Reveal Overlay   Cabinet construction in which door and drawer faces partially cover the body members or face frames of the cabinet with spaces between face surfaces creating decorative reveals.

Rift Cut   Usually referring to veneers, but can be applied to solid lumber (usually as rift sawn), this method is similar to Quarter Slicing, but accentuates the vertical grain and minimizes the "flake" of the finished material. Veneer produced by cutting at a slight right angle to the radial to produce a quartered appearance.

Riser   In stairwork, the vertical member between treads. Riser may be omitted in certain stair designs.

Rotary Slicing   Most common methods for preparing veneers for softwood plywood. The log is placed in a lathe and rotated against a stationary knife. This produces a more-or-less continuous sheet of veneer, similar to pulling a long sheet off a roll of paper towels.

Rough Cut   Irregular shaped areas of generally uneven corrugation on the surface of veneer.

Running Match   Each panel face is assembled from as many veneer leaves as necessary. Any portion left over from the last leaf may be used as the start of the next panel.

Running Trim   Generally combined in the term "standing and running trim" and refers to the trims of random, longer length delivered to the job site (e.g., baseboard, chair rail, crown molding, etc.).

Runs   In finishing, running of wet film in rivulets.

S4S   Means surfacing four sides, and generally refers to the process of reducing nominal-sized rough lumber to finished widths and thicknesses.

Sags   In finishing, partial slipping of finish film creating "curtain" effect.

Sapwood   Performs the living functions of the tree. Located just below the cambium layer. Generally lighter in color than the heartwood.

Scarf Joint   When the ends of two boards are cut on an angle and glued together to increase the length of the board.

Scribing   Drawing a line parallel with an existing surface; fitting woodwork to an irregular surface.

Sealers   In finishing, used to seal in the stain and/or filler, prior to application of the top coats.

Semi-Exposed Surfaces   In casework, surfaces which become visible when: opaque doors are open or drawers are extended; bottoms of cabinets more than 30 inches and less than 42 inches above finished floor.

Sequence Matched   When referring to paneling either:
1. Pre-manufactured sets, usually 48" x 96" or 48" x 120", numbered in sequence, and part of all or a single flitch (typically from six to twelve panels). They may be installed full width, reducing the panels at the corners or transitions; or reduced in width uniformly.
2. Sequence Matched Uniform Size sets, manufactured for the project on special order to the nearest uniform modular width practical for the installation.

3. Blueprint Matched Panels and Components, manufactured for the project on special order to achieve the maximum grain continuity since all panels, doors and other veneered components are made to the exact size required and in exact veneer sequence.

Shading   In finishing, transparent color used for highlighting and uniform color.

Shake   A separation along the grain of wood in which the greater part occurs between the rings of annual growth.

Shelf Deflection   Shelf deflection is a complex subject discussed at length in a study conducted by the Department of Wood Science at West Virginia University. (See Section 400 and 600 of the Architectural Woodwork Institute Quality Standards, Guide Specifications, and Quality Certification Program.)

Shop Drawings   See drawings.

Show Through   Irregular surfaces visible on the face of a veneered panel (such as depressions, bumps, mechanical marks, or core or frame outlines).

Slip Match   Matching between adjacent veneer leaves on one panel face. Adjoining leaves of veneer are slipped out in sequence, with all the same face side being exposed.

Softwood   Generally obtained from coniferous trees. Does not refer to the specific density or resistance to wear and abuse.

Spline Joint   When a strip of wood or compressed "biscuit" is placed into a pre-machined slot or groove and glued to reinforce and align the joint.

Stains   In finishing, produces the desired undertone color with proper distribution, depth and clarity of grain. Selection of the type of stain used is governed by the desired artistic result.

Stairwork   Wood material to form a stair, or to clad stair parts constructed of materials other than wood, and which are custom manufactured to a design for a particular project.

Standard Lacquer   In finishing, a nitrocellulose-based lacquer without additives.

Standard Trim   Generally combined in the term "standing and running trim" and refers to the trims of fixed length delivered to the job site (e.g., door jambs and casings, pre-machined window stools, etc.).

Stile and Rail Construction   Stile and rail construction for wall paneling and doors is one of the finest uses of wood as an interior finish. In custom stile and rail construction, top, cross and bottom rails run between the end stiles, and mullions run between horizontal rails; and solid lumber is selected for compatibility of color, member-to-member. In premium stile and rail construction, solid lumber is selected for compatibility of color and grain, member-to-member.

Stops   Generally, a molding used to "stop" a door or window in its frame.

Streaks, Mineral   Natural discolorations of the wood substance.

Stringer   In stairwork, member which supports and establishes the tread and riser relationship.

Substrate   Generally used to describe a panel product upon which a decorative finish material is applied.

Telegraphing   In veneer work, the variations in surface refraction as a result of the stile, rail and core show-through to the face of the panel or door. The selection of high-gloss laminates and finishes should be avoided because they tend to accentuate natural telegraphing.

Toners   In finishing, semi-transparent colors used to block out or reduce the color of wood.

Tongue and Groove   Mating groove and tongue milled into the members, generally on the edges, to improve alignment and glue surface area.

Topcoat   In finishing, the final finishing steps providing protection and the finished appearance.

Tread   In stairwork, the horizontal member which is stepped upon.

Urea Formaldehyde Resin   Commonly known as a Type I adhesive, relatively water resistant. Often requires curing by heat, but will cure at room temperature over time.

Veneer Core   Plywood constructed using a core of an odd number of veneer plies, with face and back veneers of overlays adhered thereto.

Veneering   Veneering and laminating thin pieces of wood date back to the Egyptian eras. Since that period this area of woodworking has become a highly technical business. Veneering is still common today, but production techniques have changed considerably. Modern adhesives, for example, are used instead of hard-to-handle glues.

Vinyl Lacquers   In finishing, catalyzed lacquers with a plastic rather than a nitrocellulose base.

Volute   In stairwork, a spiral or scroll end of a handrail, generally atop a newel post.

Waferboard   See particleboard.

Warp   In doors, any distortion in the door itself, measured by placing a straight edge or a taut string on the concave face.

Washcoats   In finishing, thin solutions applied as a barrier coat to wood.

Well Hole   In stairwork, the open space in which the stair is set.

White Birch   The sapwood of the Yellow Birch tree.

Windows   In architectural woodwork, all frames and sash for double hung, casement, awning, sidelights, clerestory and fixed windows. "Stock" and name brand units are not included.

Wiping Stains   Refers to pigmented oils or solvents applied to wood.

D I R E C T O R Y

Architects & Designers

Ace Architects
    David Weingarten
    Lucia Howard
330 Second Street, Suite 1
Oakland, California 94607
United States
Tel: (510) 452-0775
Fax: (510) 452-1175

Antonia Astori
Studio A. Astori
Via Rossini 3
20122 Milan
Italy
Tel: (39) 2-795005
Fax: (39) 2-76021763

Douglas Barnard
Douglas Barnard, Inc.
1443 Sixth Street
Santa Monica, California 90401
United States
Tel: (310) 458-9100
Fax: (310) 458-0019

Bedell-Laughlin & Associates
    Marjorie A. Bedell, FASID
    Lawrence G. Laughlin
6061 West Third Street
Los Angeles, California 90036
United States
Tel: (213) 930-2802
Fax: (213) 935-5132

Sara Binder
9348 Civic Center Drive, Suite 400
Beverly Hills, California 90210
United States
Tel: (310) 278-8833
Fax: (310) 278-0835

Brennan Beer Gorman Monk/Interiors
    Julia Monk, AIA, ASID
    William Whistler, AIA
    Michael Antonik
515 Madison Avenue
New York, New York 10025
United States
Tel: (212) 888-7663
Fax: (212) 935-3868

Barry Brukoff
Brukoff Design Associates, Inc.
480 Gate Five Road, Suite 310
Sausalito, California 94965
United States
Tel: (415) 332-6350
Fax: (415) 332-5968

Erika Brunson
Erika Brunson Design Associates
903 Westbourne Drive
Los Angeles, California 90069
United States
Tel: (310) 652-1970
Fax: (310) 652-2381

The Burdick Group
    Bruce Burdick
    Susan K. Burdick
35 South Park
San Francisco, Califoria 94107-1877
United States
Tel: (415) 957-1666
Fax: (415) 777-1498

Arthur de Mattos Casas
Casas Edições de Design
Rua Manuel Maria Tourinho, 46
São Paulo
Brazil
Tel: (55) 11 62 0243
Fax: (55) 11 282 6608

Centerbrook Architects
    Mark Simon, FAIA
    James C. Childress, AIA
    Leonard J. Wyeth, AIA
P.O. Box 955
Essex, Connecticut 06426
United States
Tel: (203) 767-0175
Fax: (203) 767-8719

Theodore M. Ceraldi, AIA, Architect
Theodore M. Ceraldi & Associates, Architects
P.O. Box 13
Nyack, New York 10960
United States
Tel: (914) 353-1199
Fax: (914) 914-353-1314

Steve Chase Associates
    R. Randall Patton
70-005 Mirage Cove Drive
Rancho Mirage, California 92270
United States
Tel: (619) 324-4602
Fax: (619) 328-3006

Clodagh
Clodagh Design International
365 First Avenue
New York, New York 10010
United States
Tel: (212) 673-9202
Fax: (212) 614-9125

A. J. Diamond, Architect
A. J. Diamond, Donald Schmitt and Company/
    Architects, Planners and Landscape Architects
2 Berkeley Street, Suite 600
Toronto, Ontario M5A 2W3
Canada
Tel: (416) 862-8800
Fax: (416) 862-5508

Steven Ehrlich, FAIA
Steven Ehrlich Architects
1600 Main Street
Venice, California 90291
United States
Tel: (310) 828-6700
Fax: (310) 828-7710

Rand Elliott, FAIA
Elliott + Associates Architects
6709 North Classen Boulevard
Oklahoma City, Oklahoma 73116
United States
Tel: (405) 843-9554
Fax: (405) 843-9607

Mark Enos
Enos & Co.
705 North Alfred
Los Angeles, California 90069
United States
Tel: (213) 655-0109
Fax: (213) 655-7719

John and Krista Everage
Everage Interior Design
1025 24th Street
Santa Monica, California 90403
United States
Tel: (310) 264-0066
Fax: (310) 242-0091

Hugh Farrington
P.O. Box 1516
Kihei, Hawaii 96753
United States
Tel: (808) 879-3245

J. Frank Fitzgibbons, AIA
Fitzgibbons Associates Architects
4822 Glencairn Road
Los Angeles, California 90027
United States
Tel: (213) 663-7579
Fax: (213) 663-6262

Ford, Powell & Carson, Inc.
    John Gutzler, ASID
    Peter Hinton, ASLA
    George Little, AIA
    Bonnie Bertler
    Mary Mitchell Bartlett
1138 East Commerce Street
San Antonio, Texas 78205
United States
Tel: (210) 226-1246
Fax: (210) 226-6482

Emanuela Frattini Magnusson, Architect
588 Broadway
New York, New York 10012
United States
Tel: (212) 925-4500
Fax: (212) 925-4525

Marisabel Gomez de Morales
Arquitectura de Interiores
Aurelio Ortega, #764-D
Guadalajara, Jalisco
Mexico 45150
Tel: (523) 656 2939
Fax: (523) 656 5747

Gomez Vazquez Aldana & Associates
    Jaime Gomez
    J. Manuel Gomez
Aurelio Ortega, #764
Guadalajara, Jalisco
Mexico 45150
Tel: (523) 656 4343
Fax: (523) 656 4087

Margaret Helfand Architects
    Margaret Helfand
    Marti Cowan
32 East 38th Street
New York, New York 10016
United States
Tel: (212) 779-7260
Fax: (212) 779-7758

Hemmeter Design Group
250 South Hotel Street, Suite 202
Honolulu, Hawaii 96813
United States
Tel: (808) 529-9700
Fax: (808) 529-9703

Donald C. Hensman, FAIA
Buff, Smith & Hensman
1450 West Colorado Boulevard
Pasadena, California 91105
United States
Tel: (818) 795-6464
Fax: (818) 795-0961

Agustin Hernandez, Architect
Bosques de Acacias 61
Bosques de las Lomas
C.P. 11700 Mexico, D.F.
Tel: (525) 596 1554
Fax: (525) 596 1710

Dwight Hooker, AIA
Sundance, Utah
United States

Michael La Rocca
Michael La Rocca, Ltd.
150 East 58th Street, Suite 3510
New York, New York 10015
United States
Tel: (212) 755-5558
Fax: (212) 838-3034

Joseph Minton
Joseph Minton, Inc.
3320 West Seventh Street
Fort Worth, Texas 76107
United States
Tel: (817) 332-3111
Fax: (817) 429-6111

Juan Montoya
Juan Montoya Design Corporation
80 Eighth Avenue, 16th Floor
New York, New York 10011
United States
Tel: (212) 242-3622
Fax: (212) 242-3743

Bob Moore
Bob Moore Designs
2516 Green Valley Road
Los Angeles, California 90046
United States
Tel: (213) 656-8846
Fax: (213) 656-8843

Sandra Nunnerley
Sandra Nunnerley, Inc.
112 East 71st Street
New York, New York 10021
United States
Tel: (212) 472-9341
Fax: (212) 472-9346

James W.P. Olson
Olson/Sundberg Architects
108 First Avenue South, Fourth Floor
Seattle, Washington 98104
United States
Tel: (206) 624-5670
Fax: (206) 624-3730

Luis Ortega
Luis Ortega Design Studio
8813 Rangely Avenue
Los Angeles, California 90048
United States
Tel: (310) 273-2040
Fax: (310) 273-1083

Pascal Arquitectos
    Gerard Pascal
    Carlos Pascal
Atlaltunco, #99
San Miguel Tecamachalco
Naucalpan, Estado de Mexico
C.P. 53970
Tel: (525) 294-2371
Fax: (525) 294-8513

Powell/Kleinschmidt
    Donald D. Powell
    Robert D. Kleinschmidt
645 North Michigan Avenue, Suite 810
Chicago, Illinois 60611
United States
Tel: (312) 642-6450
Fax: (312) 642-5135

Bart Prince
Bart Prince, Architect
3501 Monte Vista, N.E.
Albuquerque, New Mexico 87106
United States
Tel: (505) 256-1961
Fax: (505) 268-9045

Vishva Priya
Ahuja Priya Architects
561 Broadway
New York, New York 10012
United States
Tel: (212) 219-2122
Fax: (212) 941-1456

Cheryl Rowley
Cheryl Rowley Interior Design
9538 Brighton Way, #316
Beverly Hills, California 90210
United States
Tel: (310) 859-9185
Fax: (310) 859-8131

Samuel Sandler
314 Madero PTE
Monterrey N.L. 64000
Mexico
Tel: (528) 3 744 852
Fax: (528) 3 752 070

Sheri Schlesinger
Schlesinger & Associates
101 South Robertson Boulevard, #202
Los Angeles, California 90048
United States
Tel: (310) 275-1330
Fax: (310) 275-8698

John Seals
Davidson + Seals
13000 Skyline Drive
Oakland, California 94619
United States
Tel: (510) 531-1796
Fax: (510) 531-1798

Colin and Veronique Sharp
Box 52789 Saxonwold
2132 South Africa
Tel: (27) 11 788 4608
Fax: (27) 11 788 9909

Louis Shuster
Shuster Design Associates, Inc.
1401 East Broward Boulevard, Suite 103
Fort Lauderdale, Florida 33301
United States
Tel: (305) 462-6400
Fax: (305) 462-6408

Morlen Sinoway
Morlen Sinoway Designs
2035 West Wabansia
Chicago, Illinois 60647
United States
Tel: (312) 235-4779
Fax: (312) 235-5669

Rita St. Clair, FASID
Rita St. Clair Associates, Inc.
1009 North Charles Street
Baltimore, Maryland 21201
United States
Tel: (410) 752-1313
Fax: (410) 752-1335

Lenny Steinberg Design Associates
    Lenny Steinberg
    Melinda Ring
2517 Ocean Front Walk
Venice Beach, California 90291
United States
Tel/Fax: (310) 827-0842

Stephanie Stokes
Stephanie Stokes, Inc.
790 Madison Avenue, Suite 604
New York, New York 10021
United States
Tel: (212) 744-3379
Fax: (212) 794-9718

Stoll & Stoll
    Lucinda Wanner Stoll
    Peter Ned Stoll
3 Town Dock Road
New Rochelle, New York 10805
United States
Tel: (914) 576-0800
Fax: (914) 576-0837

The System Design
    Mark Warwick
    Kim Hoffman
9828 Charleville Boulevard
Beverly Hills, California 90212
United States
Tel: (310) 556-7711
Fax: (310) 788-3808

Tigerman McCurry Architects
    Stanley Tigerman, FAIA
    Margaret McCurry, FAIA
444 North Wells Street
Chicago, Illinois 60610
United States
Tel: (312) 644-5880
Fax: (312) 644-3750

Adam D. Tihany
Adam D. Tihany International, Ltd.
57 East 11th Street
New York, New York 10003
United States
Tel: (212) 505-2360
Fax: (212) 529-3578

Transit Design Srl
    Giovanni Ascarelli
    Maurizio Macciocchi
    Evaristo Nicolao
    Danilo Parisio
Via Emilio Morosini, 17
00153 Rome
Italy
Tel: (39) 6 589 9848
Fax: (39) 6 589 8431

Shigeru Uchida
Studio 80
1-17-14 Minami-Aoyama,
Minato-ku, Tokyo 107
Japan
Tel: (81) 3-3475-4586
Fax: (81) 3-3475-4586

David Weatherford
David Weatherford Interiors & Antiques
133 14th Avenue, N.E.
Seattle, Washington 98112
United States
Tel: (206) 329-6539
Fax: (206) 329-9348

Gary Whitfield
Whitfield Associates
1100 South Coast Highway, Suite 201
Laguna Beach, California 92651
United States
Tel: (714) 497-5466
Fax: (714) 497-3481

Mark Zeff
Mark Zeff Consulting Group
260 West 72nd Street, Suite 12B
New York, New York 10023
United States
Tel: (212) 580-7090
Fax: (212) 580-7181

Manufacturers, Suppliers & Artisans

A&Y Lumber
Provo, Utah
United States

Accent Products
5877 Rodeo Road
Los Angeles, California 90016
United States
Tel: (310) 478-5233

Alpine Log Homes
P.O. Box 85
Victor, Montana 59875
United States
Tel: (406) 642-3242
Fax: (406) 642-3242

Anglo American Cedar Products Ltd.
33286 South Railway Avenue
Mission, British Columbia V2V 4M6
Canada
Tel: (604) 826-7185
Fax: (604) 826-8594

Arte y Madera
La Calma, #30
Las Fuentes
Zapopan, Jalisco 45070
Mexico
Tel: (523) 612 7921
Fax: (523) 610 2568

Boggs-Oehler Furniture Company, Inc.
1827 McCullough
San Antonio, Texas 78212
United States
Tel: (210) 735-1432

The Bradbury Collection
8687 Melrose Avenue, G-190
Los Angeles, California 90069
United States
Tel: (310) 657-3940
Fax: (310) 657-5553

Joseph Brandi
340 Washington Avenue
New Rochelle, New York 10801
United States
Tel: (914) 272-0838

Bruce Hardwood Flooring
16803 Dallas Parkway
Dallas, Texas 75248
United States
Tel/Fax: (214) 931-3100

B+S and Lorch Woodworking
701 Whittier Street
Bronx, New York 10474
United States
Tel: (718) 991-4734
Fax: (718) 842-6759

Capitol Cabinet
252-B Lake Avenue
Yonkers, New York 10701-5783
United States
Tel: (914) 423-6464
Fax: (914) 423-4399

Clodagh Design Works
365 First Avenue
New York, New York 10010
United States
Tel: (212) 673-9202
Fax: (212) 614-9125

Condon Lumber Co.
250 Ferris Avenue
White Plains, New York 10603
United States
Tel: (914) 946-4111

David-Edward, Ltd.
Edward Hough
1407 Parker Road
Arbutus, Maryland 21227
United States
Tel: (410) 242-2222
Fax: (410) 242-0111

Decorações Bom Lar Ltda.
Rua Carnot, 677
03032 030 Canindé
São Paulo
Brazil
Tel: (55) 11 227 8117
Fax: (55) 11 943 3061

Decorative Painting
Malcolm Moorman
Renée Tinnell
1239 Keniston Avenue
Los Angeles, California 90019
United States
Tel: (213) 936-9529

Design Fabrication
1355 Lawrence, #106
Newbury Park, California 91320
United States
Tel/Fax: (805) 499-4683

Driade s.p.a.
Via Padana Inferiore, 12
Fossadello Di Caorso (Piacenza)
C.A.P. 29012
Italy
Tel: (39) 523-818660
Fax: (39) 523-822360

Duratherm Window Corporation
North Vassalboro
Maine 04962
United States
Tel: (207) 872-5558
Fax: (207) 872-6731

Duvinage
P.O. Box 828
Hagerstown, Maryland 21741-0828
United States
Tel: (301) 733-8255
Fax: (301) 791-7240

William Erbe and Sons
434½ East 75th Street
New York, New York 10021
United States
Tel: (212) 249-6400
Fax: (212) 879-8495

Eximio Móveis e Decorações Ltda.
End.: Rua Cachoeira dos Indios, 211
03818 080 Ermelino Matarazzo
São Paulo
Brazil
Tel: (55) 11 943 3061
Fax: (55) 11 227 3117

Finland Color Plywood Corporation
310 Westminster Avenue
Venice, California 90291
United States
Tel: (310) 396-9991
Fax: (310) 396-4482

Fort Hill Construction
8118 Hollywood Boulevard
Los Angeles, California 90060
United States
Tel: (213) 656-7425
Fax: (213) 654-0531

Jerry Fulks and Company
210 Third Avenue South, Suite 400
Seattle, Washington 98104
United States
Tel: (206) 624-5509
Fax: (206) 624-2925

Furnicon International Co., Ltd.
521-1 Yahata, Fujieda-shi,
Shizuoka-ken 426
Japan
Tel: (81) 54 644 7171
Fax: (81) 54 641 8181

George Geppert Lumber Company
1561 Easton Road
Roslyn, Pennsylvania 19001
United States
Tel: (215) 659-6006
Fax: (215) 659-1436

Pierluigi Ghianda & Company
20030 Bovisio Masciago (Milan)
Italy
Tel: (39) 362 590 331

Julian Giuntoli
1151 16th Street
San Francisco, California 94107
United States
Tel/Fax: (415) 863-7417

Kaare Gjerde
Gjerde Construction Co.
5947 Grizzly Peak Drive
Oakland, California 94611
United States
Tel: (510) 658-1118

Glendale Custom Cabinets
3722 A San Fernando Road
Glendale, California 91204
United States
Tel: (818) 244-3811

John Haggerty
Haggerty Woodworking
26 Church Street
Lambertville, New Jersey 08530
United States
Tel/Fax: (215) 862-5441

Eliza and Raanan Harel
Jerusalem, Israel
Tel: 972 2 630 534
U.S. contact: (310) 827-0842

Michael Haring
8946 West 25th Street
Los Angeles, California 90034
United States
Tel: (310) 839-0211

Joe Hartley
Hartley Construction
P.O. Box 1079
Makawao, Hawaii 96768
United States
Tel: (808) 572-6888
Fax: (808) 572-4133

Hartmark Cabinetry
26350 Athena Avenue
Harbor City, California 90710
United States
Tel: (310) 501-9558
Fax: (310) 325-9291

Healdsburg Lumber
359 Hudson Street
Healdsburg, California 95448
United States
Tel: (707) 431-9663
Fax: (707) 431-9655

E. W. Howell Co., Inc.
530 Fifth Avenue
New York, New York 10036
United States
Tel: (212) 944-6121
Fax: (212) 840-0418

Internacional Maderera
Camino Sta. Lucia, #397
Col. Sn. Miguel Amantla
Azcapotzalco, D.F. 02700
Mexico
Tel: (523) 811 3071
Fax: (523) 811 3071

William H. Jackson Company
210 East 58th Street
New York, New York 10022
United States
Tel: (212) 753-9400
Fax: (212) 753-7872

Frank Jones
3137 Hoomua Drive
Kihei, Hawaii 96753
United States
Tel: (808) 871-5632
Fax: (808) 871-5840

Scott Jordan
137 Varick Street
New York, New York 10013
United States
Tel: (212) 620-4682
Fax: (2120 620-5793

Kaya Builders
525 Kokea Street
Honolulu,, Hawaii 96817
United States
Tel: (808) 845-6477
Fax: (808) 845-6471

Denise Kocourek
426 Haggin Street
San Antonio, Texas 78210
United States

Peter Kramer
P.O. Box 232
Gay and Jett Streets
Washington, Virginia 22747
Tel: (703) 675-3625
Fax: (703) 675-3937

John Langenbacher Company, Inc.
1345 Seneca Avenue
Bronx, New York 10474
United States
Tel: (718) 328-7600
Fax: (718) 542-2005

M+D Flooring
          Mitchel Owen
71-A Kelawe Street
Makawro, Hawaii 96768
United States
Tel/Fax: (808) 572-5918

Martelli Associates
20 Jones Street
New Rochelle, New York 10801
United States
Tel: (914) 633-1655
Fax: (914) 633-3915

Matheny Construction
P.O. Box 1114
Gualala, California 95445
United States
Tel/Fax: (707) 884-4503

W.L. McNatt Contractors, Inc.
217 East Sheridan
Oklahoma City, Oklahoma 73104
United States
Tel: (405) 232-7245
Fax: (405) 232-7259

Melrose Lumber Co.
1201 46th Avenue
Oakland, California 94601
United States
Tel: (510) 532-8422
Fax: (510) 532-7976

Steve Miller
Miller Woodworking
14238 South Prairie Avenue
Hawthorne, California 90250
United States
Tel: (310) 978-4561
Fax: (310) 978-4727

Mueller Nicholls Co.
2400 Union Street
Oakland, California 94607
United States
Tel: (510) 444-4525
Fax: (510) 444-0752

Nachon Lumber Company, Inc.
12000 S.W. Eighth Street
Miami, Florida 33184
United States
Tel: (305) 223-2255
Fax: (305) 223-5535

NBI, Inc./Mike Beeman
12712 Carmenita Road
Santa Fe Springs, California 90670
United States
Tel: (310) 921-7067
Fax: (310) 921-5453

Niece Lumber Co.
Elm and Union Street
Lambertville, New Jersey 09530
United States
Tel: (609) 397-1200
Fax: (609) 397-2719

Pace Collection
11-11 34th Avenue
Long Island City, New York 11106
United States
Tel: (718) 721-8201
Fax: (718) 274-5530

George Pagels
2534 South Western Avenue
Chicago, Illinois 60608
United States
Tel: (312) 847-7086
Fax: (312) 847-7140

Ron Parenti
Parenti & Raffaelli
215 East Prospect Avenue
Mount Prospect, Illinois 60056
United States
Tel: (708) 253-5550
Fax: (708) 253-6055

Pella Window Co.
479 Old York Road
Jenkintown, Pennsylvania 19046
United States
Tel: (215) 576-1550
Fax: (215) 576-1964

Pittsburg Door Co.
1538 C, Willow Pass Road
Pittsburg, California 94565
United States
Tel: (510) 432-4576
Fax: (510) 432-0525

Poldo Punzo
Via Appia km. 138,9 Formia
Italy
Tel: (39) 771 772 661

Alan Reams Company
P.O. Box 380
San Marcos, Texas 78667
United States
Tel: (512) 392-0800

Eli Rios Restoration
515 West 29th Street, Fifth Floor
New York, New York 10001
United States
Tel: (212) 643-0388
Fax: (212) 643-0566

Bob Robinson Furniture
1820 Hubbard Street
Chicago, Illinois 60622
United States
Tel: (312) 733-0158
Fax: (312) 733-0159

Rosenzweig Lumber Corporation
801 East 135th Street
Bronx, New York 10454
United States
Tel: (212) 585-8050
Fax: (212) 292-8611

Santa Fe Heritage Door Co.
418 Montezuma
Santa Fe, New Mexico 87501
United States
Tel: (505) 983-5986
Fax: (505) 984-8909

Scandinavian Design
127 East 59th Street
New York, New York 10022
United States
Tel: (212) 755-6078
Fax: (212) 888-3928

Bruce Scherer
P.O. Box 961
Laguna Beach, California 92651
United States
Tel: (714) 494-2590
Fax: (714) 494-7010

Schultz Custom Cabinets
3515 Helms Avenue
Culver City, California 90232
United States
Tel: (310) 204-3407
Fax: (310) 204-3416

Sea Ranch Cabinets
P.O. Box 228
The Sea Ranch, California 95497
United States
Tel: (707) 785-2698

Serini Custom Woodworking
122 Winchester Road
Merion, Pennsylvania 19066
United States
Tel: (215) 844-7343
Fax: (215) 844-8756

Shinomiya Takezaikujo
2-3-18 Yahata, Shizuoka-shi,
Shizuoka-ken 422
Japan
Tel/Fax: (81) 54 285 1646

Philip Sicola Designs
13715 South Western Avenue
Gardena, California 90249
United States
Tel: (310) 323-8002
Fax: (310) 323-8023

Skaskiw Case and Cabinet Company
P.O. Box 100
Bridgewater, Vermont 05034
United States
Tel: (802) 672-5308

William Somerville Inc.
166 East 124th Street
New York, New York 10035
United States
Tel: (212) 534-4600
Fax: (212) 410-0236

Valente Souza Inc.
525 West 49th Street
New York, New York 10019
United States
Tel/Fax: (914) 741-2781

H. Dolin Stuart, Inc.
630 South La Brea Avenue
Los Angeles, Califoria 90036
United States
Tel: (213) 935-3995
Fax: (213) 935-3945

Summit Furniture, Inc.
P.O. Box S
Carmel, California 93921
United States
Tel: (408) 375-7811
Fax: (408) 375-0940

Taconic Builders
Attn: Jim Hanley
417 Center Avenue
Mamaroneck, New York 10543
United States
Tel: (914) 698-7456
Fax: (914) 698-6443

Bert Thomas Construction, Inc.
Sundance, Box C2
Provo Canyon, Utah 84604
United States
Tel/Fax: (801) 225-3374

Truitt & White Lumber Company
642 Hearst Avenue
Berkeley, California 94710
United States
Tel: (510) 841-0511
Fax: (510) 845-2604

Troy Wesnidge
Troy Wesnidge, Inc.
P.O. Box 239
Newcastle, Oklahoma 73065
United States
Tel: (405) 387-4720
Fax: (405) 387-9320

Western Wood Structures, Inc.
P.O. Box 130
Tualatin, Oregon 97062-0130
United States
Tel: (503) 692-6900
Fax: (503) 692-6434

Woodwork Corporation of America
1432 West 21st Street
Chicago, Illinois 60608
United States
Tel: (312) 226-4800
Fax: (312) 226-3619

Yost/Flagship Flooring
2212 Woodhead
Houston, Texas 77019
United States
Tel: (713) 526-3434
Fax: (713) 526-4660

Frank J. Zadlo Construction Services, Inc.
314 Wadsworth Avenue
Philadelphia, Pennsylvania 19119
United States
Tel: (215) 242-0412
Fax: (215) 242-0112

Photographers

Daniel Aubry
Daniel Aubry Studios
365 First Avenue
New York, New York 10010
United States
Tel: (212) 598-4191
Fax: (212) 505-7670

Aldo Ballo
c/o Antonia Astori
Via Rossini 3
20122 Milano
Italy
Tel: (02) 795005
Fax: (02) 76021763

Richard Barnes
1403 Shotwell Street
San Francisco, California 94110
United States
Tel: (415) 550 1023
Fax: (415) 957-0707

Rick Barnes
8101 Orion Avenue #4
Van Nuys, California 91406
United States
Tel: (818) 786-1756

Victor Benitez
Guanajuato - #130
Col. Roma
Mexico, D.F.
Tel: (525) 574 80 32
Fax: (525) 584 75 71

Paul Bielenberg
Paul Bielenberg Associates
2447 Lanterman
Los Angeles, California 90039
United States
Tel: (213) 669-1085
OR
6823 Pacific View Drive
Los Angeles, California 90068
United States
Tel: (213) 874 9951
Fax: (213) 874 1907

Tom Bonner
1201 Abbot Kinney
Venice, California 90251
United States
Tel: (310) 396-7125

Antoine Bootz
133 West 22nd
New York, New York 10011
United States
Tel: (212) 366-9041
Fax: (212) 366 9386

Andrew Bordwin
70A Greenwich Avenue - #332
New York, New York 10011
United States
Tel: (212) 633 0383
Fax: (212) 633 1046

Susan Lee Burdick
Susan Lee Burdick Photography
18 E. Blithedale Avenue, Suite 33
Mill Valley, California 94941
United States
Tel: (415) 388-2510

Andrew Bush
755 N. Lafayette Place
Los Angeles, California
United States
Tel: (213) 484-0367

Mario Carrieri
Via Spallanzani
Milano
Italy
Tel: (39) 2 2940 9047

Manuel Carvajal
Servicios Fotograficos
514 Circuito Azorin
Jardin Espanol
Monterey N.L.
Mexico
Tel/Fax: (528) 359 60 25

Christopher Covey
664 N. Madison Avenue
Pasadena, California 91101
United States
Tel: (818) 440-0284

Grey Crawford
1714 Lyndon Street
South Pasadena, California 91030
United States
Tel: (213) 413-4299

Billy Cunningham
26 St. Mark's Place, Apt. 4FW
New York, New York 10003
United States
Tel: (212) 677-4904

Eitan Feinholz
Atlaltunco - #99
Tecamachalco
Mexico 53970
Tel: (525) 294 23 71
Fax: (525) 294 85 13

Tim Fields
Baltimore, Maryland
United States
Tel: (410) 323-3003

Jeff Goldberg/ESTO
ESTO Photographics
222 Valley Place
Mamaroneck, New York 10543
United States
Tel: (914) 698-4060
Fax: (914) 698-1033

Janos Grapow
Via Monti Parioli 21/A
Rome
Italy
Tel: 06 32 44 831

Tim Griffith
Australia

John Hall
885 Tenth Avenue
New York, New York 10019
United States
Tel: (212) 757-0369

Jim Hedrich
Hedrich-Blessing
11 West Illinois Street
Chicago, Illinois 60610
United States
Tel: (312) 321-1151
Fax: (312) 321-1165

Agustin Hernandez
Bosque de Acacias 61
Bosques de Las Lomas
Mexico D.F. 11700
Tel: (525) 596 1665
Fax: (525) 596 1710

John Herr
220½ N. Prince Street
Lancaster, Pennsylvania 17603
United States
Tel: (717) 299-3870

Brad Hess
Brad Hess Photographer
146 Castle Heights
Upper Nyack, New York 10960
United States
Tel: (914) 358-4434

Hickey-Robertson
1318 Sul Ross
Houston, Texas 77006
United States
Tel: (713) 522 7258

Lizzie Himmel
50 West 29th Street
New York, New York 10001
United States
Tel: (212) 683-5331
Fax: (212) 683-7657

Timothy Hursley
1911 West Markham
Little Rock, Arkansas 72205
United States
Tel: (501) 372-0640
Fax: (501) 372-3366

Bruce Van Inwegen
Van Inwegen Photo
1422 West Belle Plaine
Chicago, Illinois 60613
United States
Tel: (312) 477-8344

Michael Ives
Ackerman McQueen Advertising
1601 Northwest Expressway #1100
Oklahoma City, OK 73118
United States
Tel: (405) 843-7777
Fax: (405) 848-8034

Michael Jensen
655 Northwest 76th Street
Seattle, WA 98117
United States
Tel: (206) 789-7963

Hal Lott
5320 Gulfton #8
Houston, Texas 77081
United States
Tel: (713) 661-2595
Fax: (713) 661-2597

Scott McDonald
Hedrich-Blessing
11 West Illinois Street
Chicago, Illinois 60610
United States
Tel: (312) 321-1151
Fax: (312) 321-1165

Jon Miller
Hedrich-Blessing
11 West Illinois Street
Chicago, Illinois 60610
United States
Tel: (312) 321-1151
Fax: (312) 321-1165

Steven Minkowski *(deceased)*

Michael Moran
245 Mulberry Street, #14
New York, New York 10012
United States
Tel: (212) 226-2596
Fax: (212) 226-2596

Grant Mudford
5619 West 4th Street, Studio #2
Los Angeles, California 90036
Unites States
Tel: (213) 936-9145

Michael Mundy
25 Mercer Street
New York, New York 10013
Unites States
Tel: (212) 226-4741
Fax: (212) 343-2936

Nacasa & Partners, Inc.
3-5-5 Minami-Azabu
Minato-ku, Tokyo 106
Japan
Tel: (81) 3 3444 2922
Fax: (81) 3 3444 2678

Mary E. Nichols
Mary E. Nichos Photography
132 South Beachwood Drive
Los Angeles, California 90004
United States
Tel: (213) 935-3080
Fax: (213) 935-9788

Peter Paige
Peter Paige Photography
269 Parkside Road
Harrington Park, New Jersey 07640
United States
Tel: (201) 767-3150
Fax: (201) 767-9263

Anthony Peres
645 Oxford Avenue
Venice, California 90291
United States
Tel/Fax: (310) 821-1984

Giovanna Piemonti
Via della Pilotte 21/Q
Roma
Italy
Tel: (06) 57300419

Tuca Reinés
Rua Manoell Kent, 58
São Paulo, São Paulo 045536
Brazil
Tel/Fax: 55 011 852 8735

Mark Ross
345 E. 80th #3B
New York, New York 10021
United States
Tel: (212) 744-7258
Fax: (212) 744-7258

Kim Sargent
Sargent Photography
1235 U.S. Highway One
Juno Beach, Florida 33408
United States
Tel: (407) 627-4711
Fax: (407) 694-9078

Leslie Schwartz
2147 N. Claremont
Chicago, Illinois 60647
United States
Tel: (312) 276-3210

Colin Sharp
Box 52789
Saxonwold 2132
South Africa
Tel: (11) 788 4608
Fax: (11) 788 9909

Kevin Smith
2035 West Wabansia
Chicago, Illinois 60647
United States
Tel: (312) 772-1113
Fax: (312) 772-1747

Tim Street-Porter
2074 Watsonia Terrace
Los Angeles, California 90068
United States
Tel: (213) 874-4278

Philip Thompson
1109 Longwood Avenue
Los Angeles, California 90019
United States
Tel: (213) 939-6307
Fax: (213) 931-2523

Peter Vitale
P.O. Box 10126
Santa Fe, New Mexico 87504
United States
Tel: (505) 988-2558 (212) 888-6409
Fax: (212) 838-7369

Paul Warchol
Paul Warchol Photography
133 Mulberry Street - #6S
New York, New York 10013
United States
Tel: (212) 431-3461
Fax: (212) 274-1953

Alan Weintraub
Alan Weintraub Photography
2325 Third Street, Suite 325A
San Francisco, California 94107
United States
Tel: (415) 553-8191
Fax: (415) 553-8192

Toshi Yoshimi
Toshi Yoshimi Photography
4030 Camero Avenue
Los Angeles, California 90027
United States
Tel: (213) 660-9043
Fax: (213) 660-2497

INDEX

Photographers

A C K N O W L E D G M E N T S

Having benefitted twice before from its high standards in the publication of *Empowered Spaces* (now released as *At Home & At Work*) and *Furniture: Architects' & Designers' Originals*, I am thrilled to have the opportunity to write four more books for PBC International, Inc. Conceived as a series on the residential use of tile, stone & brick; wood; glass; and fabrics, their development could not have been possible without the extraordinary commitment of Publisher Mark Serchuck and Managing Director Penny Sibal to good design. That Managing Editor Susan Kapsis has overseen and scrutinized their development fills me with a sense of security. Besides, with our interests being similar and our enthusiasm high, we have had a marvelous time!

PBC's Technical Director Richard Liu has again lent his expert analysis to make sure that only excellent photographic material prevails. And Garrett Schuh's design, sensitive to the subject, has kept me in a constant state of excitement. The art department's Barbara Ann Cast proved indispensable to the final execution of the layout. And to the editorial department's Francine Hornberger, Dorene Evans and Donna Ahrens, for perfecting every detail — a million bouquets! I was also most grateful to have had James Gabrie, Beatrix Jakots Barker and Tuula Stark come to my aid when I was desperately in need of translators, and to have had the admirably thorough Angeline Vogl proofread every word.

The list grows as I try to remember the many people who have supported this endeavor as I have called their offices across the United States and throughout the world. Among those who have been especially helpful with this volume are Joseph A. Sorelli and Judith B. Durham of the Architectural Woodwork Institute, and Regis Miller of the United States Department of Agriculture, Forest Service, Forest Products Laboratory.

I am grateful to the many architects, designers and photographers whose work fills the pages of this book, as well as to the homeowners who have so generously shared their living spaces for publication. And finally, I am indebted to Stanley Abercrombie for graciously contributing the foreword which appears in each of the four books in the series.

dar California Redwood Red Oak Lodgepole Pine Cedar Honduras Mahogany

ne White Oak Butternut Red Alder Walnut Rock Maple Eastern White Pine I

ropean Walnut Amaranth European Cherry Akatio White Birch Teak French V

ne Western Red Cedar California Redwood Red Oak Lodgepole Pine Cedar Ho

d Alder Amaranth American Black Walnut Rock Maple Eastern White Pine Eng

ropean Cherry Akatio White Birch Teak French Walnut White Ash Macassar E

White Oak Butternut Red Alder American Black Walnut Rock Maple Eastern W

ropean Walnut Amaranth European Cherry Akatio White Birch Teak French V